Walt Disney World Dining Guide 2019

Katherine Walsh

Theme Park Press
The Happiest Books on Earth
www.ThemeParkPress.com

Theme Park Press is not associated with the Walt Disney Company.

The views expressed in this book are those of the author and do not necessarily reflect the views of Theme Park Press.

Theme Park Press publishes its books in a variety of print and electronic formats. Some content that appears in one format may not appear in another.

Editor: Bob McLain
Layout: Artisanal Text

ISBN 978-1-68390-174-7
Printed in the United States of America

Theme Park Press | www.ThemeParkPress.com
Address queries to bob@themeparkpress.com

Contents

Introduction

To all who come to this hungry place, welcome. You are about to consume the most up-to-date and delicious version of the *Walt Disney World Dining Guide*. This year's edition will include many new restaurants, counters, and kiosks, as well as updates to your old favorites.

"You're going to Walt Disney World...again?" This is a question I've gotten from co-workers, cousins, neighbors, and my dad. It's hard to answer, so I rely on what's probably pretty close to the truth: I'm going back because of the food. In the past five years, I've been to Walt Disney World around twenty times, and I have not even come close to scratching the surface—especially when it comes to the world-class dining. I still have restaurants I want to visit, ones where I'd like to return, and new restaurants are constantly popping up.

As with most things, dining preferences are subjective. Your server could recommend that the tuna tartare on their menu is the best they've ever had. However, this wouldn't mean much to you if you aren't into seafood. With this in mind, I will do my best to stay reasonably objective in order to provide you with the perfect amount of information for you to be able to make informed decisions on what you choose to eat at Walt Disney World.

That being said, there are certain places at Disney World that the majority of guests tend to love or loathe. You well may be in the minority and enjoy a restaurant that most people think is awful. It doesn't make you wrong. It makes you human. However, I do not plan on steering you wrong by recommending dining locations that aren't worth your time and money. A great vacation at Disney World can hinge on the ability to manage your time and get the most bang for your buck. I am here to tell you which places you should make a reservation and (perhaps more importantly) which locations to avoid. Keep in mind that this is just one girl's viewpoint, but it is a girl who has eaten a lot of what Disney World has to offer.

Let's start with an unofficial glossary of dining terms you'll see a lot of in this guide:

- **Advanced Dining Reservations (ADRs).** These are dining reservations that you can (and should) make in advance long before your trip to Disney. ADRs can be made online or by calling (407) WDW-DINE. They can be managed on the My Disney Experience mobile app or the Walt Disney World website.

- **My Disney Experience (MDE)**. The mobile and web application that controls your vacation right from your personal device. Some like it, some hate it, but it's increasingly an essential part of your Disney World trip.

- **Table Service.** A restaurant where you are seated by a host, order off a menu, and have a server. At the conclusion of this meal, you will tip said server.

- **Quick Service.** A meal where you order from a cast member, (or via mobile ordering through My Disney Experience) and then your food is brought to you on a tray at the ordering counter. You are tasked with finding your own table for quick-service locations; and if it's a prime eating time, you may be hard-pressed to find a spot to sit.

- **Character Dining.** Meal experiences, usually buffets, where Disney characters roam about the restaurant. Character meals tend to skew to the younger demographic—mainly families with kids. This is a good way to guarantee a photo opportunity with your favorite Disney character.

- **Disney Dining Plan (DDP).** This is a pre-paid addition to your vacation package if you are staying on Disney World property during your trip.

- **Tables in Wonderland (TiW).** A dining discount card for annual passholders, Disney Vacation Club members, and Florida residents. This handy-dandy card costs $150–$175 (depending on your affiliation to one of the aforementioned groups) for 13 months and gives you 20% off food and beverage (including alcohol!) at participating dining locations.

- **The Disney Check.** Nope, this isn't the sinking feeling you get in your stomach when you reconcile your credit card statement after a Disney vacation. The Disney Check, which used to be called the Mickey Check, helps families identify meals that are more balanced and nutritious for their children.

- **Mickey Bars.** You can find these little treats all over WDW. Perhaps the most pervasive of the Disney snacks, they are vanilla ice cream bars on a stick with a hard chocolate shell shaped like Mickey Mouse's head.

- **Churro.** A popular Disney snack. If you are reading a Disney dining guide, you've probably come toe-to-toe with one of these fried dough pastries..

- **Dole Whip.** Another unique Disney snack. A Dole Whip is a pineapple-flavored soft-serve treat. It is only served at a few select spots in Disney World. Disney fans go gaga over Dole Whips.

- **Nuggets, Burgers, and Fries.** This isn't a widespread term, but it's my book, so my rules. Disney has a lot of food courts and counter-service options that sell a homogenized mix of the same chicken nuggets, burgers, and fries. I'm not crazy about these spots, because I think that Disney can do better. We'll refer to these as nuggets, burgers, and fries spots.

- **Rope Drop.** The phenomenon of families and friends waking up really early (even though they are on vacation) to get to a theme park right at opening, in hopes of beating the rest of the crowd into the park.

- **Extra Magic Hours (EMH).** Extra Magic Hours are a perk for guests staying on Disney property, allowing them to enter the theme parks early or stay later than the general population not staying on property.

Think for a moment about your vacation identity. Are you the kind of person who thinks their time spent in a Disney park is precious and the less time spent sitting down in a restaurant and being waited on the better? Are you a parent who has a picky eater for a child? Are you a parent who *is* the picky eater of your group? Are you adventurous, wanting to try any and all new food and drink while on vacation? Lucky for you, all these tastes are accounted for and celebrated in Disney World.

My plan for the book is to travel to all four theme parks, Disney Springs, and the Boardwalk. Then, I'll highlight the best of the specialty dining at the resorts. I'll give you a broad overview of the menu and insert any of my personal preferences along the way, so even if our tastes differ, you will know what kind of cuisine to expect at any given restaurant.

But first, a few words about the dining reviews you'll encounter in this book, and then an overview of the Disney Dining Plan.

About the Dining Reviews

In the following chapters, I indicate the cost of eating at each Disney quick-service or table-service restaurant with a range of prices:

* $14.99 and lower
** $15-$34.99
*** $35-$59.99
**** $60 and higher

Depending on how finicky you are, you can enjoy a good meal at the low end of the range or splurge on the high. Of course, Disney frequently changes its prices, usually upwards, so if cost is a crucial factor in your decision to eat at a specific restaurant, check the menu beforehand. For up-to-the-minute, guaranteed accurate information, check only the menus on the official Walt Disney World website. Use the menus on Disney fan sites with caution, as they're often out of date.

Unless otherwise indicated, the cost range is per adult. If the restaurant offers a Tables in Wonderland discount, you'll see the designation "TiW" after the cost range.

The credit "cost" for each meal is designated with "S" (Snack), "Q" (Quick Service), or "T" (Table Service), depending upon what kind of Disney Dining Plan (DDP) credit it requires.

Reservations are *always* recommended at table-service restaurants. At the more popular ones, like Cinderella's Royal Table, 'Ohana, and Chef Mickey's, reservations might as well be *required*, as they're snapped up quickly. (At some venues, like Disney's dinner shows, reservations really *are* required.)

During less busy seasons, you might get lucky as a walk-up and score a table. It never hurts to try. But if you know your dining plans in advance, avoid possible disappointment and book a reservation.

The dining reviews are ordered by location. Usually, there are snack items available at locations designated as accepting quick-service credits, so when you see a venue listed as "quick service," assume that you can use snack credits there, too, for some items. In contrast, table-service locations rarely, if ever, have snack items available. Food kiosks and stores that sell food items, whether eligible for the dining plan or not, are organized at the start of each section. A few venues are not on the dining plan; their reviews are placed wherever it makes sense to put them.

Now that we've dispensed with the appetizers, let's move on to the main course.

CHAPTER ONE

Disney Dining Plan

The Disney Dining Plan is an add-on to your vacation if (and only if) you're staying at a Walt Disney World resort. There are three variations of the plan. Some include more table-service meals while others focus more on the grab-and-go meals.

- The **Quick Service Dining Plan** costs $52.50 per adult per night (of hotel stay) and $23.78 for children. Per day, it includes two quick-service meals, two snacks, and one refillable resort mug that can be filled for the length of your stay.

- The **Regular Dining Plan** costs $75.49 per adult per night and $27.98 per night for children. This plan includes one table-service meal per day, one quick-service meal per day, two snacks per day, and a refillable resort mug.

- The **Deluxe Dining Plan** costs $116.25 per adult per night and $43.49 per night for children. This includes three meals per day (you can choose between quick service and table service), two snacks per day, and a refillable resort mug.

A note about the refillable resort mug. These little beauties can be found at any of the resort food courts/counter-service eateries on property. They are 16 oz. insulated plastic mugs containing RFID chips that are activated at the beginning of your stay. You can also purchase these mugs separately from the dining plan. The current cost for a standalone mug is $18.99 for the length of your stay. Each resort's food court has a fountain of Coke products, coffee, and a little sink for you to wash out your mugs. The mugs are not valid for any in-park refills besides ice water. However, they are valid for other resorts. So, if you are staying at Pop Century but know you'll be at the Polynesian for lunch, you can fill your mug there! Some of the larger resorts have multiple locations sprinkled around the resort to fill up your mug. Don't worry about bringing it back the next time you vacation; because of the RFID chip, you won't be able to use it past your departure.

Each of the dining plans offers a combination of credits, redeemable for your food items whether it be a sit-down meal or a scoop of popcorn. Some of the more upscale and in-demand Walt Disney World restaurants require two dining credits in exchange for a meal. Those restaurants are:

- Cinderella's Royal Table in Magic Kingdom
- Le Cellier Steakhouse in Epcot
- Monsieur Paul in Epcot
- The Hollywood Brown Derby in Hollywood Studios
- Tiffins in Animal Kingdom
- Jiko in the Animal Kingdom Lodge
- Flying Fish on the Boardwalk
- California Grill in the Contemporary
- Cítricos in the Grand Floridian
- Narcoossee's in the Grand Floridian
- Spirit of Aloha Dinner Show at the Polynesian
- Artist Point in Wilderness Lodge
- Yachtsman Steakhouse in the Yacht Club
- Hoop-Dee-Doo Musical Revue at Fort Wilderness
- Mickey's Backyard Barbeque at Fort Wilderness
- Morimoto Asia in Disney Springs
- STK Orlando in Disney Springs
- Paddlefish in Disney Springs
- The BOATHOUSE in Disney Springs
- In-room dining at the resorts as well as pizza delivery also cost two dining credits.

There are a few restrictions to the Disney Dining Plan, most notably, Victoria & Albert's in the Grand Floridian. You cannot use DDP credits here. It's more than a meal, it's an experience. You'll have to pay out of pocket for Victoria & Alberts, but more on that later. Also, none of the restaurants in the Swan and Dolphin hotels are included in the Disney Dining Plan (and there are some excellent restaurants in the Swan and Dolphin!).

If you are opting-in for the Disney Dining Plan, the same plan must be purchased for all members of the resort reservation. Mom and Dad can't get the deluxe plan and expect the kids to eat scraps of their meals. It also must be purchased for the entire resort stay, so you can't just pick the middle three days of your trip to get in on the dining plan. It's all or nothing. If you opt-in, you get however many nights you are staying at your resort. You also must decide before check-in if you are participating in the DDP.

The Disney Dining Plan seems to cater to a group that loves convenience. Just scan your MagicBand, and your meal is taken care of. Your DDP credit is deducted from your account. Disney isn't in the business of saving you money or offering you tons of free food. Dollar for dollar, the DDP tends to be a little more expensive than if you order off the menu. Usually, Disney offers the dining plan for free once a year. On the day you can begin booking the free dining plan, you will find the website down and travel planners taking calls frantically from their clients. Here's the catch: if you get in on the free dining plan, no other discounts are available. It's worth your money to compare dollar for dollar. Another note about the DDP's convenience is the ability to use dining plan credits by mobile ordering.

The plan also caters to another group: people who are hungry. You get *a lot* of food on the DDP. I've only done the DDP once, and I walked away from every meal feeling uncomfortably full. Also, on the last day of my trip, I had so many leftover snacks I was grabbing bags of chips and water bottles to take with me on the airplane.

Don't get me wrong. I'm not trying to talk you out of the DDP. I think it works for a particular set of travelers. I'm just not sure I'm one of those travelers. My favorite time of year to visit WDW is in the fall during Epcot's International Food & Wine Festival. Disney should offer a special "Food and Wine" dining plan during this time of year, because most of the items are small plates (snack credits) and I find myself not eating a traditional meal when I'm food and wining—I just eat tons of offerings from the kiosks. I would waste the quick-service and table-service credits at this time of year.

Cancellations

This seems like an appropriate time to talk about Disney's dining cancellation policy. In order to cancel a dining reservation with no penalty, it must be done the day before the reservation. Otherwise, you are charged $10 per person on the reservation. The same goes for no-shows. (Victoria & Albert's is an even more costly cancellation fee.)

Now, a somewhat unscrupulous loophole to get around the cancellation fee is to move your reservation a few days into the future. Once you do this, you will be able to cancel your reservation online without penalty. I don't feel guilty about letting you in on this secret, as it opens up the reservation for someone else. You're sprinkling a little pixie dust on someone's day! This rationale is paired with the fact that a lot of people *don't* know about ADRs before they visit Disney World. I was once one of these people, pathetically wandering around Epcot in search of any sit-down restaurant for my last night of vacation. I only let that happen once before I learned. If you're a real Disney villain, loiter around Cinderella's Royal Table while the host tells unsuspecting parents they should've done their research six months ago. This is why I think you should be able to cancel reservations sooner than a day before. These restaurants are in demand, and Disney knows it. There's no need to create undue exclusivity. If I don't want to eat in the castle an hour before my meal, by all means, give it to the dad who is sweating bullets trying to explain to his daughter (who is dressed like Cinderella) that Cosmic Ray's Starlight Café is basically the same thing as eating in the castle. But this won't be you, because you are armed with this book.

Special Requests

When you book your reservation on Disney's website, be sure to look at the fine print and make any special dietary requests.

Disney is *very* sensitive to dietary needs/restrictions and allergies. Many restaurants ranging from quick service to sit-down have special menus available upon request. I've heard tales of Disney going as far as to calling families before vacations to touch base regarding restrictions, or head chefs of the restaurants paying a special visit to the table to make sure everyone is comfortable with their order. If you forget to do this when you book your reservation initially, you can tell your server.

A Dining Hack

I'll let you in on a Disney hack. While all the restaurants on Disney property take ADRs made through the Disney World website, there *are* other means of making reservations. OpenTable.com offers booking at many of the WDW restaurants on property, including Flying Fish, Jiko, Kona Café, Morimoto Asia, Paddlefish, and Enzo's Hideaway. Try it if the Disney website is being fickle or if you want to search other available time slots.

CHAPTER TWO

Magic Kingdom

The Magic Kingdom is synonymous with Walt Disney World. It's the original Disney World theme park, opening in 1971. It's the most fantastical of the parks, where you can follow the Seven Dwarfs down their mine, help a pirate pillage, or watch Tinker Bell soar over the castle on her nightly flight. It doesn't matter if you're a kid or just a kid-at-heart, there is something *magical* about the Magic Kingdom. (I know, I'm a real wordsmith.) Even though it is the smallest of the Disney parks in Florida, it has the highest attendance of any theme park in the world, with over 20 million guests passing under the train station in 2017. While it's not known for the quality of its dining, if you look hard enough, you can find some tasty treats.

Main Street, U.S.A.

Main Street embodies what I love about Disney—the details. This is a place where you can sit and watch the world go by, and you are bound to notice something new every time you visit. As you walk down Main Street, take in the sights, sounds, and smells. Look for the nods to the Disney imagineers and their contributions to the Disney company on the windows of the Main Street buildings. As you walk by the ice cream parlor, take a deep breath and smell the delicious aroma wafting through the air. Even though this is the land with the fewest attractions, I urge you to make the most out of your time on Main Street.

Kiosks, Wagons, and Carts

Most of the wagons and carts found in the park sell Dasani water bottles, so I won't specifically mention them again. At press time, a bottle of Dasani water sells for $3 on Disney property.

The Main Street Ice Cold Refreshment Cart and Town Square Ice Cream Cart sell a variety of ice cream treats, including the ever-present Mickey bar. It also sells frozen bananas and the Olaf Frozen Lemonade-Strawberry Bar. There are several stops on Main Street to indulge in my personal favorite Disney park snack, popcorn! Who can resist the smell of freshly popped buttery popcorn. Throughout the year, Disney releases special popcorn buckets. Sometimes they are refillable (if you are a popcorn fan like me, this is a pretty good deal) or they feature Disney characters that fit the season. For example, Oogie Boogie from *The Nightmare Before Christmas* served as a past Halloween bucket character.

Casey's Corner
DDP: One credit (Q)/Cost: $
TYPE: American; Quick Service; Lunch and Dinner

This stop is about as American as it gets—eating a hot dog, in a baseball-centric eatery, in a Disney park. The location is themed around the short "Casey at the Bat" (which was itself based on the famous poem by Ernest Thayer) from the Disney animated feature *Make Mine Music*. The menu features a variety of hot dogs, from the standard all-beef hot dog and to the more adventurous mac and cheese all-beef hot dog topped with, you guessed it, mac and cheese. And bacon. Forever bacon. My favorite item on the menu is the corn dog nuggets. They are delicious and portable. The fries here are really good as well. They aren't like the rest of the French fries you get at other quick-service spots. It could be that you can drench them in nacho cheese. Cheese makes everything better. Now may be the time to mention you won't find any Disney Check meals here. Another downside is the seating situation. A very limited number of seats are available inside, and they're located at the back of Main Street's massive and high-traffic gift shop, the Emporium. If you plan your meal at Casey's carefully, you can time it with the piano player performances outside the restaurant near the outdoor seating. The pianist plays lively ragtime tunes that enhance the overall experience of Main Street. Casey's also participates in mobile ordering, so you can bypass the typically long line here.

Main Street Bakery
DDP: One credit (Q)/Cost: $
TYPE: American; Quick Service; Snacks

A few years ago, Starbucks invaded Walt Disney World. You will find a Starbucks location in each of the four parks, and this one is the Magic Kingdom's. You'll be able to order the same specialty drinks available at your local Starbucks. In addition, you'll find breakfast sandwiches and baked goods. You can also collect Starbucks rewards with your purchases, but you cannot redeem them here or anywhere else on Disney property.

Plaza Ice Cream Parlor
DDP: No / Cost: $
TYPE: American; Quick Service; Snacks

At the end of Main Street, close to the hub, you will find the best way to end your night at the Magic Kingdom: hand-scooped ice cream. Here you'll find an array of ice cream sundaes, cones, and ice cream sandwiches in a variety of flavors. They even have some fat-free and no-sugar-added treats. If you are up for the challenge, the Mickey's Kitchen Sink Sundae is available. This treat is served in a "sink" reminiscent of Mickey's red shorts. You'll get a little taste of everything: chocolate, vanilla, and strawberry ice cream; hot fudge, strawberry, and caramel sauces; and chocolate and peanut butter chips. Topped with whipped cream and cherries, the sink is meant to be shared, but I'm not judging you if you eat this by yourself. In fact, I'm impressed. The kitchen sink costs $16.99.

Crystal Palace
DDP: One Credit (T) / Cost $$-$$$ (TiW)
TYPE: American; Character Buffet; Breakfast, Lunch, and Dinner

On the walkway toward Adventureland you will find a dazzling building modeled after London's 1851 Great Exhibition that housed the first World's Fair. Inside, you'll see a white interior with high glass ceilings and plants taking in the natural light. A keen eye will also notice costumed characters from Winnie the Pooh. Well, I mean, even a non-keen eye will notice that. For this character dining, you'll find your favorite Hundred Acre Wood friends: Winnie the Pooh, Tigger, Piglet, and Eeyore.

Breakfast, lunch, and dinner are all served buffet-style, and kids in your party will have their own "mini-buffet" featuring mac and cheese and chicken fingers. Perhaps unfortunately, the mini-buffet is called "Pooh Corner" (please, Disney, I beg you, change the name, before kids start getting ideas...). Adults will find the typical breakfast fare of waffles, pancakes, breakfast meats, and a "make your own omelette" station. For lunch and dinner, there's a carving station, chicken, fish, pasta, peel-and-eat shrimp, and a variety of desserts. They also serve a few bottles of domestic beer and wine by the glass or bottle.

The Main Street Confectionary
DDP: No/ Cost $
TYPE: American; Quick Service; Snacks

A passerby might think this is just a gift shop filled with coffee mugs and kitchen wares. However, it's a great spot to buy Disney specialty treats and candies. You'll find a mix of character-themed cookies, lollipops, Rice Krispie Treats, bulk candies, fudge, and other confections in the display case. You can find these treats at other places on property, but the unique thing about the confectionary is that you can watch cast members making them in the back of the shop. Sometimes, as you pass through, you might even find a cast member holding out a tray with samples. Never, *ever* pass up the sample trays.

The Plaza Restaurant
DDP: One credit (T) / Cost: $$ (TiW)
Type: American; Casual; Lunch and Dinner

Bridging the gap between Tomorrowland and Main Street, just past the Plaza Ice Cream Parlor, you'll stumble across the Plaza Restaurant. It's a bit more tucked away than the rest of the Main Street sit-downs. The style inside is Art Nouveau, with mirrored walls and a solarium. The menu is informal, with an emphasis on home-cooked meals like meatloaf, a grilled Reuben, a club sandwich, and a fried green tomato sandwich. You can start and end your meal with a refillable milkshake. Disney Check meals include a turkey sandwich and a PB&J sandwich on honey-wheat bread. Wine and beer are also served here. A common Disney dining hack of old was that you could dine at a restaurant for lunch and get a reduced cost for the same exact food served at dinner. Sadly, this hack is being phased out, and it's evident at the Plaza, where the prices are the same whether you're eating lunch or dinner there.

Tony's Town Square

DDP: One credit (T) / Cost: $$ (TiW)
TYPE: Italian; Casual; Lunch and Dinner

You'll find this eatery at the base of Main Street adjacent to the Town Square Theatre where you can meet Mickey and Tinker Bell. Tony's is modeled after the scene in *Lady and the Tramp* where the titular characters share their first plate of spaghetti and kiss over the swelling melody of "Bella Notte." Ah, if only the food here was that romantic.

The food at Tony's is meh, but the location is great, so of course people fill the restaurant. The patio overlooks the hustle and bustle of Town Square and Main Street. This is not where you should go if you are looking for good Italian food. But, if you think—"Hey, I really like *Lady and the Tramp*, and I want to eat with a view of Main Street"—this is your place. But, let's talk about the food, which includes Italian staples like ravioli, fettuccini alfredo, spaghetti, and pizza, and for dessert, tiramisu, cannoli, and gelato. The Disney Check entrées are whole wheat spaghetti with turkey meatballs, grilled chicken with roasted potatoes, and sautéed shrimp with whole wheat spaghetti. There's a moderately sized wine menu and a few Italian beers like Peroni and Moretti.

In 2014, my husband and I had a trip planned with our best friends, another couple, Erin and Joe. We were celebrating Joe's 30th birthday and right before the trip, Erin told us that she was pregnant. Her morning sickness was in full swing on our trip, and nearly everything she ate made her sick. The only place that did not make her sick was good ol' Tony's Town Square. Do with that information what you will.

Tomorrowland

A few steps from the Plaza Restaurant, you'll find yourself as far away from the turn of the century as you can be...the future! There's a great big beautiful tomorrow shining at the end of every day, and Tomorrowland is the home of all things futuristic, sci-fi, and out of this world. Stop to take your photo in front of the Instagram-worthy purple wall before you enter the land that's home to Space Mountain and Buzz Lightyear's Astro Blasters. In my opinion, Tomorrowland is the weakest of all the themed lands in the Magic Kingdom as far as food is concerned. Tomorrowland does not house any table-service meals. All of its food offerings are either quick service or snacks.

Tomorrowland Kiosks, Wagons and Carts

The Cool Ship stand in Tomorrowland sells hot dogs and churros. If Tomorrowland is really busy, you may notice Space Dog, a cart selling primarily hot dogs, also in operation. You'll also find carts scattered around with frozen treats and popcorn. I mentioned Starbucks when we spoke about Main Street, but it's important you become familiar with Joffrey's as well. Joffrey's is the other coffee brand of Walt Disney World. If you stay on property, this is the brew you'll find for your in-room coffee maker. Aside from that, Joffrey's also has in-park kiosks selling a variety of coffee and tea drinks, and of course delicious pastries. One of these kiosks is in Tomorrowland—Joffrey's Revive. If it's a hot day, go for the peach iced tea or the frozen cappuccino (this is my favorite; it's pure sugar). They also have specialty lattes on the menu, like the Dreamsicle iced latte and the dulce de leche iced latte.

Auntie Gravity's Galactic Goodies

DDP: No / Cost: $
TYPE: American; Quick Service; Snacks and Breakfast

If you aren't into the hand-scooped ice cream of Main Street, here's the spot for you. Auntie Gravity specializes in soft ice cream and floats. In addition to their fixed menu, Auntie is oft home to specialty or seasonal items. At press time, there is an Incredibles 2 promotion going on in Tomorrowland, and you can find Edna's "No Capes, Just Crepes" crepe sundaes at Auntie Gravity's.

Cosmic Ray's Starlight Café
DDP: One credit (Q) / Cost: $
TYPE: American; Quick Service; Lunch and Dinner

Cosmic Ray's is the largest eatery in Tomorrowland, running parallel to the Tomorrowland Speedway, closest to Fantasyland. Ray's is organized into three "bays"—this used to matter when you would line up depending on your order, but they've since combined the menus. Bays or no bays, It's a stereotypical nuggets, burgers and fries place. The food is made without love and the menu is so homogenized that there's nothing that's "uniquely Cosmic Ray's Starlight Café." Well, except for Sonny Eclipse, but you can't eat him. Sonny Eclipse is an alien lounge singer with too wide of a smile and too-small feet. Over the course of the day, he performs a 27-minute jazz music/lounge act set in the seating area of Cosmic Ray's. The instrument he plays is called an astro organ. He's from Yew Nork City on Planet Zork, and his backup singers are called the Space Angels, and oh, they're invisible, because...Cosmic Ray's.

The Lunching Pad
DDP: One credit (Q) / Cost: $
TYPE: American; Quick Service; Lunch and Dinner

At the base of the Astro Orbiter, you'll find the Lunching Pad. It features a menu of hot dogs and BBQ pork sandwiches. I've now come to understand that it seems that hot dogs are the food of the future, or at least the unofficial food of Tomorrowland. The Lunching Pad is home to my favorite thing to eat in Tomorrowland: a warm pepperjack-stuffed pretzel. The restaurant participates in mobile ordering, which is great for someone like me who is just a gal wanting a stuffed pretzel. The seating is often crowded during peak times during lunch and dinner, and it's all outdoors so this may not be ideal on a hot day.

Tomorrowland Terrace Restaurant
DDP: One Credit (Q) / Cost: $
TYPE: American; Quick Service; Lunch and Dinner

You'll find this eatery tucked away on the walking path from Main Street (near the Plaza) to Tomorrowland. It's open seasonally, and the seating area is a covered terrace that has a great view of Cinderella Castle—so great, in fact, that the dessert viewing party for fireworks is housed here. As for their regular operating menu, you'll find burgers and an assortment of Asian cuisine, including a pulled pork banh mi sandwich with a spicy sriracha aioli and an Asian salad with five-spice pork. For kids, a Smuckers Uncrustable makes the cut for the Disney Check meal. This location offers mobile ordering with the My Disney Experience App.

Fantasyland

It's tough to ignore the magic of Fantasyland—unless it's 1p.m. and you find yourself navigating a parking lot of strollers. Seriously, avoid Fantasyland in the afternoon. I'll put my cynicism aside to say that Fantasyland is the most fantastical of all the lands and draws on childhood nostalgia with the Disney animated classics. This is where you can fly over London with Peter Pan, eat in the West Wing with Beast, and go under the sea with Ariel. It doesn't get much better than that.

Fantasyland Kiosks, Wagons and Carts

Fantasyland expanded in 2012, and with that expansion came a plethora of new goodies to eat. The Storybook Circus big top is a large gift shop you won't be able to miss. Inside, you'll find Big Top Treats, serving sweet treats ranging from cotton candy, house-made caramel corn, and chocolate dipped fruits, including strawberries, pineapples, and bananas. If sweet popcorn isn't your thing, head on over to Maurice's Amazing Popping Machine for traditional popcorn cooked up by the hair-brained but lovable father of Belle. You'll find another popcorn stand in the Storybook Circus area, as well as a pretzel stand. There are also several ice cream carts dotted around Fantasyland. Prince Eric has a village market that's only open seasonally, selling items like hummus, fruit, and pickles. Food fit for a prince.

Be Our Guest Restaurant

DDP: One credit (T) / Cost: $-$$ (TiW for dinner only)
TYPE: French; Unique/Themed; Breakfast, Lunch, and Dinner

This is one of those restaurants you are going to want to camp out at exactly 180 days to snag a reservation. It's one of the most popular restaurants in Walt Disney World. Be Our Guest is unique in that it's a quick service for breakfast and lunch, but a table service for dinner—and it's the only quick service on property where you can (or must) make reservations. Be Our Guest is in the back of Fantasyland at the base of Beast's Castle. Once inside, take note of the beautiful attention to detail. For instance, the Imagineers replicated the snowfall pattern from *Beauty and the Beast* that appears in the large window.

There are three distinct dining areas. The first, called the West Wing, is where you'll see the enchanted rose and catch a glimpse of the Beast's transformation during a storm. There's also the Ballroom, the largest of the eating areas, and the romantic Rose Gallery, where you can see the elegant statuette of Belle and the Beast dancing above the tables.

For breakfast, you'll see a more refined menu—no Mickey waffles to be found here. You can try the Feast a la Gaston, with scrambled eggs, herb-roasted potatoes, apple smoked bacon, and sausage served with fresh fruit and pastries. This is how Gaston gets "roughly the size of a barge." You can also get scrambled egg whites or a croissant doughnut.

At lunch, you order on automated kiosks and find a seat. You'll grab your own silverware and drink and a server will bring your lunch to you. The potato leek soup is one of their signature items, but my favorite is the French dip sandwich. The bread is a delicious French baguette, and like Casey's, the French fries (ahem, I'm sorry)—*pomme frites*, are not your typical Disney fries. You should also end every meal here with the master's cupcake—the grey stuff, it's delicious!

Dinner is more upscale and elegant than breakfast or lunch. The lights are dimmed and the whole restaurant seems less noisy. Dinner at Be Our Guest is the most difficult reservation to obtain. You will see charred octopus and escargot listed for appetizers. There's filet mignon, lamb chops, and pork tenderloin. Be Our Guest broke the mold and was the first location in the Magic Kingdom to serve alcohol, though it's served only during dinner. You'll find wines from Napa and France, champagne, and domestic and imported beers.

I am going to make a bold prediction here. Get in on Be Our Guest while it's still only one DDP credit. I think within the next few years it will be two. It has sustained its popularity since it opened in 2012. The hours have expanded to include breakfast, and you used to be able to just walk up for lunch without a reservation—not anymore! Even though dinner is not considered character dining, after your meal you are encouraged to meet-and-greet the Beast.

Cheshire Café

DDP: One credit (S) / Cost: $
TYPE: American; Quick Service; Snacks and Breakfast

This café is found at the crossroads of Fantasyland and Tomorrowland, near the teacups. How else is the coy Cheshire Cat able to keep tabs on Alice? You'll find an assortment of juices, slushies, and coffee. For food, there's a ham and cheese pretzel (similar to a stromboli) and the Cheshire Cat Tail. The Cheshire Cat Tail is what we call an Instagram snack. It's a long pastry with bright pink and purple frosting that is just oh-so photogenic. Seating is limited—there are a few small tables beneath umbrellas.

Cinderella's Royal Table

DDP: Two credits / Cost: $$$-$$$$ (TiW)
TYPE: American; Character; Fine/Signature; Breakfast, Lunch, Dinner

I know I said Be Our Guest was a hard-to-get dining reservation, but Cinderella's Royal Table might be *the* most difficult-to-get reservation in Walt Disney World. Why? Location, location, location. For this experience, you are dining *in* Cinderella Castle *with* Cinderella (well, not *with* Cinderella, but you do get to meet her and get your photo taken with her). The other princesses you might encounter are Ariel, Aurora, Belle, Jasmine, and Snow White, or at least some combination of them. All of the meals are fixed price, and you must pay in full upon booking your reservation.

At breakfast, you'll start with assorted pastries, then choose an entrée such as a traditional breakfast with eggs, breakfast meat, and potatoes; a healthy choice with oatmeal; a multigrain croissant with avocado, shrimp and grits; caramel apple-stuffed French toast; beef tenderloin and egg; and baked quiche. Cheese frittata is the Disney Check meal, but kids can also choose between a traditional breakfast, cereal, and a royal children's breakfast with waffles, sausage, and fruit. There are mimosas, bellinis, and sangria for adults at breakfast.

The same menu is offered for lunch and dinner. For starters, you will choose between the soup of the day, salad, or a charcuterie plate. Then, you'll pick an entrée: braised pork shank, vegetable couscous, beef tenderloin salad, beef and shrimp, pan-seared all-natural chicken, or the chef's fish of the day. As a grand finale, there are desserts ranging from cheesecake, chocolate mousse, citrus chiffon cake, and lemon sorbet. Children have more Disney Check choices than they do at breakfast: turkey pot pie, seared fish of the day, and roasted chicken leg. The alcohol options are expanded for lunch and dinner to include champagne, wine, and beer.

The moral of the story is that if you want to eat in a medieval banquet hall with your favorite princesses, you better be on it 180 days out, because once people get this reservation, they hold onto it—cancellations are rare.

Gaston's Tavern
DDP: One credit (S) / Cost: $
TYPE: American; Quick Service; Lunch and Dinner

No one is as slick or as quick as Gaston, or makes the same caliber cinnamon rolls. At Gaston's Tavern, you'll find sweet and savory items, such as a ham and brie sandwich or a smoked turkey with swiss and cranberry sandwich. Snacks include a chocolate croissant, the aforementioned world-famous cinnamon roll, and an assortment of veggies and fruit. Most people come to Gaston's for his sidekick LeFou's drink, LeFou's Brew. It's made of frozen apple juice with a hint of toasted marshmallow and topped with all-natural passion fruit-mango foam. The décor inside Gaston's is worth checking out as well—you'll see a manly lair filled with antlers (duh), animal pelts, and more of Gaston's stunning achievements. If you step outside the tavern, you might see the man himself, Gaston, flexing his muscles and wooing the ladies.

Pinocchio Village Haus

DDP: One credit (Q) / Cost: $
TYPE: Italian; Quick Service; Lunch and Dinner

This Pinocchio-themed eatery is situated next to "it's a small world." In fact, there's a seating area that overlooks the happiest cruise that ever sailed. The haus offers flatbreads, pasta dishes like chicken parmesan and penne with marinara, and chicken nuggets. The Disney Check meal here is a Smuckers Uncrustable. Kids also have their option of flatbreads as well as macaroni and cheese.

There is quite a bit of indoor and outdoor seating at Village Haus. Heed the same warning I gave to Fantasyland as a whole—this place is swarming with people during meal times. The tables always seem dirty, with food on the floor and a lot of frantic-looking parents. It might be worth your while to pick another quick-service location in the Magic Kingdom.

Storybook Treats

DDP: One credit: (S) / Cost: $
TYPE: American; Quick Service; Snacks

Satisfy your sweet tooth at Storybook Treats! The menu ranges from the basic soft-serve ice cream to a cookie sundae with hot fudge and sprinkles on a chocolate chip cookie. They also have a hot fudge sundae, strawberry sundae, and floats with your choice of fountain beverage. Another Instagram-worthy snack lives here, the Peter Pan float consisting of lime soft serve, Sprite, and a red chocolate feather.

The Friar's Nook

DDP: One credit (Q) / Cost: $
TYPE: American; Quick Service; Lunch and Dinner

This oft-overlooked spot has an interesting menu that is constantly changing. Next to Storybook Treats, I could see how someone would think this is just an extension of the ice cream window. Currently, the Friar's Nook is all-in on tater tots: loaded buffalo chicken tots, loaded Greek tots, and loaded fiesta tots. You can also purchase a hot dog with tots. Keep your eye on the menu, and you might find a unique item that's being market-tested. (R.I.P. Pot Roast Mac & Cheese.)

Liberty Square

Liberty Square may not be the flashiest of the Magic Kingdom's lands, but it certainly has character. This quaint land is the smallest in the park and is meant to look like colonial America. The Hall of Presidents, Haunted Mansion, and the Muppets' Great Moments in History are the only attractions and shows in Liberty Square, but you would be doing yourself a disservice if you didn't explore this land thoroughly.

Liberty Square Kiosks, Wagons and Carts

Popcorn, ice cream, and hot dogs (and sometimes pizza) are available most days in Liberty Square. Does this surprise you? Be sure to take note of the Liberty Square Market next to the Hall of Presidents where you will find fruits, veggies, and chips, as well as other options that tend to be more on the healthy and fresh side. Eating nothing but essentially fast food on your vacation when you typically eat a well-balanced diet can catch up to you. Take a healthy eating break here.

Columbia Harbour House

DDP: One credit (Q) / Cost: $
TYPE: American; Quick Service; Lunch and Dinner

I realize I've been a bit tough on the quick-service locations in the Magic Kingdom. I know how well Disney can do and it's sad when they seemingly don't put effort into making the menus unique and worthwhile for repeat visits. I will, however, change my tune on Columbia Harbour House. If you're looking for decent quick service dining that's not all the same nuggets, burgers, and fries, look no further than Columbia Harbour House. That's not to say chicken nuggets don't grace this menu, but there are other options for our no-nugget brethren. Columbia Harbour House is technically in both Fantasyland and Liberty Square, across from the Haunted Mansion's gift shop, Memento Mori.

The combo platters on the menu are shrimp and fish with hush puppies, fried shrimp with nuggets and fish, and finally nuggets and fish solo. I usually opt for a sandwich here. My favorite is the tuna sandwich on multigrain bread, but the lobster roll is also worth mentioning. There's a chicken salad, a shrimp salad, and for the health-conscious eater, grilled salmon. Disney Check meals are Smuckers Uncrustables, a garden salad with chicken, and the tuna sandwich. End your meal with a slice of Boston cream pie or seasonal cobbler.

This two-story establishment has plenty of seating. My favorite seating area is upstairs in the area where passersby walk under the restaurant to get to Liberty Square or Fantasyland. It seems more quiet and relaxing than other quick-service dining in the Magic Kingdom. This location also offers mobile ordering.

Liberty Tree Tavern

DDP: One credit (T) / Cost: $$ (TiW)
TYPE: American; Casual; Lunch and Dinner

The atmosphere of Liberty Tree Tavern is modeled after a colonial inn, and each of the rooms is themed around a historical figure in United States history. Time your meal right, and you might have a prime vantage point to watch the Festival of Fantasy Parade.

For lunch at Liberty Tree, you've got choices, and it all depends on your hunger level. You can go for the "All-You-Care-To-Enjoy Bill of Fare" or order from the menu a la carte. The all-you-care-to-enjoy includes the Declaration Salad, Ooey Gooey Toffee Cake for dessert, and the Patriot's Platter for the main course. What does a patriot eat, you may ask? Roasted turkey breast, pot roast, oven-roasted pork with mashed potatoes, seasonal vegetables, stuffing, and mac and cheese is the answer, my friend. If you order off the menu, your options are pot roast, fish and chips, pasta with chicken, a grilled chicken salad, a cheeseburger, and pasta with shrimp. The dinner menu is limited to the all-you-care-to-enjoy option. The Disney Check meals are oven-roasted turkey and pasta. There are also children's portions of the pot roast and macaroni and cheese. There are three domestic beers (Sam Adams is a draft!) and a variety of wines from California.

Sleepy Hollow Refreshments

DDP: One credit (S) / Cost: $
TYPE: American; Quick Service; Snacks

I would describe funnel cakes as a lot of things. Refreshing wouldn't be one of them. However, I'm willing to look past that for a taste of one of these delightful treats. Sleepy Hollow is located to the right of the entrance of Liberty Square if you are entering through the hub. They have an item on their menu, the breakfast egg and cheese waffle sandwich, that is only available until noon. Another savory item that you can order here is the sweet and spicy chicken waffle sandwich. Waffles and funnel cakes are the linchpin, served with strawberries, powdered sugar, and chocolate hazelnut spread. Recently, Sleepy Hollow added a churro ice cream sandwich to their menu. That's right, a glob of ice cream in between two flat churros.

There are a few seats located against the wall nearest the castle. If you can grab one of those for parade or firework time, hold on and don't let go. You'll have a great view of both. Also, a fair warning that the waffles and funnel cakes are made fresh, so you might have to wait a few minutes for your order. Be patient—the wait is worth it.

Frontierland

Themed after America's Old West, Frontierland is home to two of the most thrilling rides in the park: Big Thunder Mountain Railroad and Splash Mountain. The details aren't lost in the thrills, though. It wouldn't be out of place to catch a guest wearing a coonskin cap while tapping their foot to the tune of Country Bear Jamboree.

Frontierland Kiosks, Wagons, and Carts

Churros, hot dogs, popcorn, and ice cream are all staples of any good Disney land. Luckily, you'll find all of these treats along the streets of Frontierland—sometimes more than once! Seasonally, you might also find turkey legs. Grab a snack and relax on the banks of the Rivers of America.

Prairie Outpost

DDP: No /Cost: $
TYPE: American; Quick Service; Snacks

If you aren't looking for the Prairie Outpost, you might miss it. It's tucked away right next to Pecos Bill's. If you have a hankering for a pre-packaged snack, this is your place. They have Goofy's candy, Chip 'n' Dale snack bags, Minnie's sweets, and some homemade goods like caramel apples and decorated cupcakes. May I suggest going to the Main St. Confectionary instead? Same thing, but better.

Westward Ho Refreshments

DDP: No / Cost: $
Type: American; Quick Service; Snacks

This small hut resembles a log cabin and sells breakfast (bacon, egg, cheddar, and pepper jack on a croissant) and lunch/dinner (a corn dog and trail mix). The menu's small, but you can also find refreshing beverages like cold brew coffee and lemonade slushies.

Golden Oak Outpost

DDP: One credit (S) / Cost: $
TYPE: American; Quick Service; Snacks

Golden Oak Outpost is to Frontierland what Friar's Nook is to Fantasyland. It's always worth checking out because you never know when the menu changes. (Like when the whole menu was waffle fries.) Sometimes the outpost is open, sometimes it's closed, sometimes it's open seasonally. At press time, the menu consists of chicken nuggets, chili queso fries, jalapeño poppers, cauliflower, and waffle fries.

Pecos Bill Tall Tale Inn and Café

DDP: One credit (Q) / Cost: $
TYPE: Southwestern/Mexican; Quick Service; Lunch and Dinner

No, this isn't just the place where they dump you out after seeing the Country Bears. It's also one of the very few decent quick-service eateries in the Magic Kingdom. You'll find an extensive menu filled with rice bowls, fajitas, tacos, lettuce wraps, salads, nachos, and for all you traditionalists—cheese-burgers. I'm not above ordering a cheeseburger here because you can customize it at the world-famous toppings bar. For kids, a scaled-down version of the adult menu is available with rice bowls, nachos, and burgers. For Disney Check, there's a veggie rice bowl and, you guessed it, a Smucker's Uncrustable. There's plenty of indoor seating for those hot days, and you can usually find room for a large party in the back of the dining room in air conditioning. You can use mobile ordering at this location.

The Diamond Horseshoe

DDP: One credit (T) / Cost: $
TYPE: American; Casual; Lunch and Dinner

I'm glad the Diamond Horseshoe finally has something going for it. I've seen this location closed, serving only quick foods, open seasonally, and host to weird dance parties featuring Lady Tremaine, the stepsisters, and the Country Bears. In its current state, the Diamond Horseshoe is an all-you-care-to-enjoy dining spot with down-home cookin'.

For lunch, you can order off the menu or opt for the saloon feast. The feast consists of a mixed greens salad, potato salad, watermelon salad, beef brisket, grilled chicken, corn on the cob, barbeque pulled pork, macaroni and cheese, barbeque baked beans, coleslaw, and a dessert trio with buttermilk chocolate cake, peaches and cream cheesecake, and seasonal berry cobbler. Phew. If none of that suits your fancy, you can order a sandwich featuring pulled pork, brisket, or chicken. Then there are the Chuck Wagon Platters that come with pork, brisket, or chicken and fix'ins. For dinner, you are strictly limited to the saloon feast. Children get the same feast as adults for a discounted price. Doesn't sound like anyone will be leaving here hungry. They have a variety of wines and beers, and (fun fact!) the Diamond Horseshoe is the only place in the Magic Kingdom where they have installed a draft system for pouring beers.

Adventureland

Welcome to the jungle. Explore the lush and exotic land that is Adventureland. Here you'll hear birds sing words and flowers croon, watch pirates sacking towns and things, and catch a sight of the famous backside of water.

Adventureland Kiosks, Wagons, and Carts

Of course you'll find popcorn and ice cream in the Adventureland carts. But you'll also find the most amazing snack in the entire Magic Kingdom—the cheeseburger egg roll. Yes, it's exactly what it sounds like, and it's every bit as delicious as you can imagine. You can find these little beauties to the right of the steps you descend to get to the Jungle Cruise. Follow your nose to the popcorn cart or treat yourself to glazed almonds, which are for purchase in Adventureland, too.

Aloha Isle

DDP: One credit: (S) / Cost: $
TYPE: American; Quick Service; Snacks

Located next to the exit of the Enchanted Tiki Room, Aloha Isle is home of the Dole Whip—one of the most iconic Disney snacks. You can get your Dole Whip in a float with pineapple juice or just plain in a cup. Go for the classic pineapple or get the vanilla swirl, the choice is yours! If you like Dole Whip but want more substance, treat yourself to the pineapple upside-down cake served with pineapple Dole Whip. You might find a longer line here than you do at some of the Magic Kingdom's attractions—thankfully, Aloha Isle has mobile ordering.

Jungle Navigation Co. Ltd. Skipper Canteen

DDP: One credit (T) / Cost: $$ (TiW)
TYPE: African/Asian/Latin; Casual; Lunch and Dinner

We'll call this the Skipper Canteen for short, and it's the only table-service dining option in Adventureland. This is the home for Jungle Cruise skippers off the clock—and this time, they're bringing their humor to you, tableside. There are three dining areas: the Mess Hall, the Secret Meeting Room of the Society of Explorers and Adventurers, and the Jungle Room.

The menu is more exotic compared to other Magic Kingdom menus. You'll see the skipper's sense of humor shine through with items like "Tastes like Chicken" Because It Is!, "A Lot at Steak" Salad, and Baa Baa Berber Lamb Chops. Disney Check Meals include Tiki Tiki Shrimpy Shrimpy, Smiley's Little "Croc" (chicken and pasta soup), seasoned steak, and Congo Connie's Coconut Curry Concoction. The appetizers shouldn't be overlooked either (the shumai is my favorite). There's a large wine selection for those over 21. The Skipper Canteen also serves a variety of domestic and imported beer. Try the Kungaloosh, an African-inspired deep amber ale brewed exclusively for Walt Disney World. There are also two specialty cocktails on the menu: a house-made spiced sangria and the Jungle Navigation Co. Shandy.

I've found that it's easy to get reservations at the Skipper Canteen. I'm not sure a lot of people a) know where it's located or b) like the looks of the menu. As you enter Adventureland from the hub, you'll find the canteen on your right as you pass under the Adventureland archway. Coming from a person who was an extremely picky eater as a child, there's no way my parents would've taken me here—but it would've been their loss, because Skipper Canteen is a truly unique, fun dining experience in the Magic Kingdom.

Sunshine Tree Terrace

DDP: No / Cost: $
TYPE: American; Quick Service; Snacks

Unique to Adventureland, Sunshine Tree Terrace is a place where fruity and tropical ice cream treats live. Try one of their floats, like the Citrus Swirl Float with classic frozen orange juice slushy and vanilla soft serve with orange soda or the Orange Cream Float with Dole orange soft-serve. You can also order plain vanilla soft-serve here.

Tortuga Tavern

DDP: One credit (Q) / Cost: $
TYPE: Southwestern/Mexican; Quick Service; Lunch and Dinner

This seasonally open restaurant has a very limited menu. For both lunch and dinner, you can order ribs, a turkey leg, or a hot dog (with or without chips). The dining area is directly across from the entrance to Pirates of the Caribbean and is only open on the Magic Kingdom's most busy days.

Since it's seldom busy, Tortuga serves two alternative purposes. One is overflow seating for Pecos Bill. The second is the hub for players of the interactive Magic Kingdom game, Sorcerers of the Magic Kingdom. Sorcerers young and old gather at Tortuga with their spell cards hoping to complete their sets, and sharing trade secrets. (If you have more questions about Sorcerers of the Magic Kingdom, stop by the firehouse on Main Street. Tell them Merlin sent you.)

CHAPTER THREE

Epcot

Walt Disney's original concept for Epcot was an Experimental Prototype Community of Tomorrow where citizens would work, live, and play within the same community. When Walt died, this concept was tweaked into the theme park known today as Epcot. Even though this wasn't the original vision of Epcot, since its opening in 1982, it has been delighting fans with its unique blend of futurism, culture, and fun. Epcot is a park where crowd level matters very little. Even if it's packed, there's plenty of room to roam around and having a good time is not contingent upon getting on tons of rides (like it is at the Magic Kingdom).

Epcot has two distinct areas: Future World and World Showcase. Future World is where you'll find the geodesic sphere (or giant golf ball), Spaceship Earth, which serves as the park's icon. World Showcase is the home of all the country pavilions (eleven in total)—a stretch of land measuring a mile that surrounds the body of water called the World Showcase Lagoon.

Future World Kiosks, Carts, and Wagons

You'll need nourishment and energy in order to conquer all of Epcot. Good thing you have plenty of grab-and-go options as you explore Future World. Before you even enter the park, under the monorail station, you'll find a Joffrey's Coffee stand. My favorite for hot days is a frozen cappuccino—it satisfies both my caffeine and my sugar cravings. You'll find popcorn and frozen treats on both sides of Future World. In addition to your typical PopSecret movie theater butter-flavored popcorn that you can purchase all over the parks, there's also a cart by the Imagination pavilion that sells specialty flavors, like cheddar and buffalo. Over by the Land Pavilion, you'll see a cart that serves fresh fruit and other healthy snacks.

Taste Track

DDP: One credit (S) / Cost: $
Type: American; Quick Service; Snacks

Located between Mouse Gear and Test Track, this location serves a variety of specialty ice cream treats. The Chocolatey Churro Sundae is vanilla ice cream with hot fudge, topped with whipped cream, chocolate curls, and a churro. There's an Apple Pie Sundae with vanilla ice cream and caramel sauce, topped with whipped cream, caramel popcorn, salted caramel pearls, and warm apple pie. The Berry Explosion Sundae comes with pound cake, whipped cream, and cotton candy. It might be wise to ride Test Track *before* stopping here.

Electric Umbrella

DDP: One credit (Q) / Cost: $
TYPE: American; Quick Service; Lunch and Dinner

Electric Umbrella is located near the fountain across from the biggest gift shop in Epcot, Mouse Gears. It saddens me that people eat here on a daily basis. You are exploring the park with the best food options and you pick this nuggets, burgers, and fries place? Don't be fooled by the Disney website's depiction of this eatery. It is not somewhere you would order a piece of blackened salmon over greens. Nuggets. Burgers. Fries. I think my parents took me here when I was a kid. I was a super-picky eater and I'm sure that was part of their rationale, but please, even if someone in your party is picky (and they don't want to eat in the World Showcase), at least show them you care by taking them to Sunshine Seasons (see below). Disney Check meals are Smucker's Uncrustables and a turkey sandwich on honey-wheat bread. There's also an assortment of desserts and cupcakes. Come for the nuggets, burgers, and fries—stay for the air conditioning.

Fountain View

DDP: One credit (Q) / Cost: $
TYPE: American; Quick Service; Snacks and Breakfast

This is Epcot's Starbucks location. To the right of the fountain (hence the name), you will find this spot raised above the crowd and serving your favorite lattes, mochas, and macchiatos. Breakfast sandwiches are served daily until they run out, and you may even find some non-Starbucks Disney pastries.

Sunshine Seasons

DDP: One credit (Q) / Cost: $
TYPE: Global; Quick Service; Breakfast, Lunch, and Dinner

My pick for the best counter service on property. This eatery is located in the Land Pavilion, in between the entrances for Living with the Land and Soarin'. It boasts a wide variety of fresh choices. You will find a few different counters from which to order—one is a counter with an Asian theme, another is a grill, another serves sandwiches, another soups and salads. The entrées come with a listed side, but no worries if that's not your cup of tea—you can swap it out for one of the other sides. The Mongolian beef is one of my favorites. My husband goes for the fish tacos every time we visit. I also enjoy the slow-roasted pork loin; the portion size is extremely generous. In fact, if you compare it side-by-side to the "Hardy Har Char" Siu Pork that you can buy at the Skipper Canteen in Magic Kingdom, you will notice that the portion at Sunshine Seasons is much bigger, and nearly half the price. Disney Check meals are salmon, chicken wraps, drumsticks, and Uncrustables. Kids can also order mac and cheese, pasta with meatballs, and grilled cheese. Make sure you save room for dessert as there are many offerings, like mousse cake, crème brûlée, strawberry shortcake, cheesecake, cookies, brownies, cupcakes, and whoopie pies.

The seating area for Sunshine Seasons is located in a high-traffic area, so beware if you're looking to grab a table during peak lunch or dinner hours. Even though you're close to the hustle and bustle in the Land Pavilion, I find that the atmosphere of the restaurant is more upscale than other quick-service locations. The space has an open air feeling with soaring banners overhead.

Sunshine Seasons also serves breakfast. The menu ranges from the healthy (breakfast power wrap with wild rice, sweet potatoes, blueberries, avocado, and tofu, or overnight oats) to the sinful (cinnamon rolls, cinnamon French toast bread pudding, or a breakfast croissant sandwich).

Coral Reef Restaurant

DDP: One credit (T) / Cost: $$ (TiW)
TYPE: Seafood/American; Unique/Themed; Lunch and Dinner

I would totally lose my late 80s/early 90s kid credibility if I didn't mention my love of this restaurant simply based off the episode of the TV show *Full House* where the gang visits WDW. In my eight-year-old eyes, this restaurant was the most fancy, romantic place that could ever exist. Watching fish as you eat fish? MIND. BLOWN.

Coral Reef is attached to the Seas Pavilion next to the Nemo and Friends ride. The best part is the huge (and I mean huge) salt-water aquarium that makes up one of the walls of the restaurant. This is the same aquarium you can view from the Seas Pavilion—it's the largest indoor salt-water environment ever built. Keep tabs on the sharks and fish that call this tank home. When you check in at the host stand, you can request a seat near the tank, but it's not guaranteed. I've seen guests throw full-on adult tantrums at the host stand when they are told the disappointing news that their request can't be honored. Remember, you are more likely to be accommodated if you are friendly and understanding. Plus, any seat in this restaurant has a good view of the tank—it does take up an entire wall.

Coral Reef has its fair share of bad reviews that include both food and service problems, but I've never experienced them. I'll add a disclaimer: I am not a fish eater. So, when I go to Coral Reef, I tend to order steak—which isn't a problem, because the menu offers enough non-seafood options to cater to everyone.

The lunch and dinner menus feature the same food and pricing. Begin your meal with soup, salad, calamari, shrimp cocktail, or ravioli. For the main course, seafood lovers can choose from lobster mac and cheese, mahi mahi, salmon, and shrimp and grits. Landlubbers can choose from tempura-fried cauliflower, oven-roasted chicken breast, bone-in pork chop, and sirloin steak. Additions include lobster tail, Crab Oscar, and shrimp skewers—you can't order these in conjunction with the DDP. The kids' menu is a little more grown-up with items like grilled fish of the day (Disney Check), grilled chicken with soy sauce, pasta with parmesan cream sauce, shrimp and grits, a steak, and turkey sloppy joes (Disney Check). Round off your meal with turtle cheesecake, key lime tart, warm vanilla custard filled strudel, angel food cake, the Chocolate Wave, or Baileys and Jack Daniel's mousse. If you're looking for an alcoholic beverage, there are several mixed drinks (most feature rum, and are more tropical in nature), beer, and wine.

Garden Grill

DDP: One credit (T) / Cost: $$-$$$ (TiW)
Type: American; Character Buffet; Breakfast, Lunch, and Dinner
Spin round the Land with Mickey, Pluto, Chip, and Dale. This restaurant slowly turns above the Living with the Land attraction. You can overlook the scene with the desert, prairie, and the charming farmhouse complete with barking dogs and crowing roosters. Since this is a "restaurant in the round" and every table has an outward view of the ride scenes, the tables and seating are very limited. If it's your plan to dine here on your trip, book it ASAP. By the time the restaurant makes one full rotation, you should have had ample time to finish your meal, and to meet, greet, and get a photo op with all the characters. If you're a fan of Soarin', you can strategize your morning reservation to get into the park before the rest of the guests, beating the rope drop crowd to the Soarin' queue.

It's only right that Garden Grill looks down on Living with the Land, because their menu includes fresh options—some of which are grown right in the Land Pavilion. For breakfast, it's the all-you-care-to-enjoy Chip 'n' Dale Harvest Feast. It includes Chip's sticky bun bake, fluffy scrambled eggs, thick-sliced bacon and sausage links, fresh fruit, hash brown-style potato barrels (tots), and Mickey-shaped waffles. The meal is family-style, and adults and children share the same menu for breakfast—you are charged depending on your age. If you're still hungry after the first serving, ask for more. You paid for it! Adults can also get mimosas (orange *or* raspberry).

The lunch and dinner menus are the same in both content and price. At press time, they are clocking in at $47.93 for adults and $28.76 for children. The food choices include a harvest-inspired farmers salad, turkey breast, pot roast, carved pork, French fries, mashed potatoes, veggies, stuffing, mac and cheese, and a berry shortcake for dessert. The price of your meal includes a non-alcoholic beverage, but you can buy alcoholic beverages separately—beer, wine, sangria, and even a specialty drink, the Citrus Freeze with orange vodka, peach Schnapps, and mango puree.

Club Cool

DDP: No / Cost: $
Type: American; Quick Service; Snacks

Even though you can buy snacks and sodas at Club Cool, it's not the main reason for visiting. Club Cool is sponsored by Coca-Cola, and they have fountains of soda from around the world for you to try. From the good (Inca Kola from Peru), the bad (Grecian Fanta), to the ugly (Beverly, Italy, woof). The best part about this tasting experience is that it's free of charge. Who said nothing's free at Disney? Even the sticky floor is included. It's baptism by fire for any Disney vet to take unsuspecting first-time-visiting friends and family to taste Beverly for themselves—extra bonus points if you don't tell them it's disgusting beforehand.

In addition to taste-testing the world's colas, you can also buy Coke merchandise and frozen Coke slushies. Also for purchase are candy bars, items from Minnie's Sweets line, and Goofy's candy.

Let's continue our magic journey through Epcot and dip our toes into *my* favorite part, World Showcase. This is where you bear witness to the most prime eating and drinking you can do on WDW property. Typically, World Showcase opens at 11:00am. That's when all the shops and restaurants open—which is why you'll find most of the food options to be lunch- and dinner-centric. There are a few exceptions, of course, and we'll talk about them in turn.

World Showcase: Mexico

Mexico Kiosks, Wagons, and Carts

Joffrey's coffee locations are all over World Showcase, and one of them is near the entrance to Mexico selling hot or frozen coffees, specialty drinks, and pastries that would make Homer Simpson drool. Even though I may suggest stopping at Joffrey's in the Magic Kingdom for a little pick-me-up when your energy is lagging, I don't recommend the same in Epcot. There are so many other places to eat and drink that it seems like a waste to me to get homogenized coffee (the same that you can brew in your hotel room if you're staying on property) and doughnuts.

La Cantina de San Angel

DDP: One credit (Q) / Cost: $
TYPE: Mexican; Quick Service; Lunch and Dinner

It's a trying task for even a veteran Disney fan to know the difference between all the "San Angels" in Mexico. You've got the cantina, the hacienda, and the inn. When planning your meals in Mexico, make sure it's for the *right* San Angel.

La Cantina is Mexico's quick-service option. It's located at the mouth of the World Showcase and you will often see long lines and crowds here at peak times, which is unfortunate, because it creates a bottleneck getting into the World Showcase. The menu features classic Mexican options like tacos, nachos, empanadas, and salads. I enjoy the food here. It's simple, and if you aren't hitting it right at lunch or dinner, it's a great spot to just go in and get an order of nachos to share.

The seating is open air under a pavilion of sorts. It's a great location to watch Epcot's nighttime spectacular, IllumiNations, but not the best spot on a hot day. Also, there always seem to be birds begging for food here. Don't feed the animals, folks.

Choza de Margarita

DDP: No / Cost: $
TYPE: Mexican; Snack

This is the newest edition to the Mexico pavilion. Choza is located across the path from La Cantina. It's essentially a quick service for margaritas and small Mexican plates: tacos, guacamole, and empanadas. The food is fresh and authentic. The tortillas are corn, not flour, and you are given a lime and a side of corn relish with the tacos and empanadas. They have frozen and on-the-rocks margaritas and even a few Mexican beers on the menu. The seating is outside with some tree cover, but incredibly limited. On a really hot day, I'd probably opt for Cava instead. I suppose it all depends on what you're looking for. Food? Choza. Drinks? Cava. (More on La Cava in just a bit.)

La Hacienda de San Angel
DDP: One credit (T) / Cost: $$
TYPE: Mexican; Unique/Themed; Dinner

The next San Angel on our list. La Hacienda is just past the cantina as you enter the World Showcase. It's the most upper-echelon of all the Mexican eateries. Themed to look like you are on a Mexican estate, the food is authentic and made fresh daily. You might find a few more unique choices on this menu than you will on the menu of San Angel Inn.

La Hacienda only serves dinner. The appetizers on the menu are guacamole, empanadas, crema de elote, queso fundido, and flautas. There are a few entrées that serve two, like La Hacienda, which includes grilled New York strip, chicken breast al pastor, chorizos, veggies, beans, and esquites, or Del Mar, which includes grilled shrimp, scallops, fish, vegetables, beans, and esquites. Entrées for one include tacos, snapper, New York strip, braised short ribs, and chicken breast. Kids can choose from grilled chicken, chicken tenders, cheese quesadillas, and mac and cheese. La Hacienda has a ton of adult drink options like margaritas, wine, and tequila flights. You will also find traditional Mexican desserts on the menu like flan and apple empanadas.

La Hacienda is on the water which makes it ideal for watching IllumiNations. Not all of the tables face the windows, so beware if that's your goal.

La Cava De Tequila
DDP: No / Cost: $
TYPE: Mexican; Snack

This loosely translates to "the tequila cellar." It may be my favorite spot in all of Walt Disney World. First, I love the inside of the Mexico Pavilion. I love how it's always nighttime, it's cool, and it smells like really delicious food and Disney water. Oh, how I love the smell of Disney water: one part water, one part chlorine, with just a sprinkle of pixie dust. La Cava is located on the right side of the inside of the pavilion. It's pretty easy to miss. I had been going to Disney World a few years as an adult and I never knew of this hidden gem. The one thing that gives La Cava away is the typically long line.

La Cava has a great social media presence and they have an item on their menu called the "Twitter Shot" which is $3 off normal price if you show them you're following them on Twitter. (@cavadeltequila) Even though their tequila list is beyond impressive, I most love the margaritas. My favorite is the avocado margarita, a smooth blend of avocado with tequila and rimmed with hibiscus salt. The cucumber margarita with pineapple juice and basil is also quite refreshing on a hot day.

While there is an inside area where you can sit down and order drinks, there isn't much availability, so if you're in a hurry or with a larger-sized party, stand in line and get a drink to go. The service is great, and the wait staff works quickly to get patrons (and Patron) in and out. If you do get one of the coveted tables inside, they have a limited food menu with chips, salsa, guacamole, and queso.

San Angel Inn Restaurante

DDP: One credit (T) / Cost: $$ (TiW)
TYPE: Mexican; Unique/Themed; Lunch and Dinner

This is the San Angel *inside* the pyramid. It's always nighttime at the San Angel Inn—probably so you don't get a good look at your food. I kid, I kid (kind of)...

I already said the inside of the Mexico Pavilion is one of my favorite places in Disney World, so *ipso facto*, the restaurant inside should be one of my favorites, right? Wrong. A few years ago, when my husband and I were fresh out of college and kind of broke, we went for a meal at the San Angel Inn. It was one of our only dining reservations for a five-day Disney trip (see: we were broke). I was looking forward to it, and it was a huge disappointment. You're paying for the atmosphere here, guys. The food is mediocre, as is the service. There was a tray next to us which sat with half-eaten, not-yet-bussed-back-to-the-kitchen food on it the entire time.

The menu has tacos, carnitas, carne asada, salmon, salads, and sautéed shrimp. There are two chef recommendations: a combo platter where you get a small sample of many of the entrées, and a catch of the day. For dessert, there's dulce de leche, Mexican sorbets, cheesecake, and flan. The children's menu is exactly the same (content and price) as that of La Hacienda. They offer a selection of margaritas, including my favorite, avocado, also found at La Cava. You might need more than one to enjoy this meal.

All joking aside, I would be willing to try the San Angel Inn again. Maybe we had a bad server. Maybe it was an off-day. I don't think you can completely write something off having only been there once, but it does pain me to think people are paying high prices for mediocre meals. Disney can do better.

World Showcase: Norway

Norway Kiosks, Wagons, and Carts

Right outside of Anna and Elsa's Royal Sommerhus, you will find a beer cart serving, you guessed it—beer! You can also buy Mickey ice cream bars here. Wouldn't the Olaf treat fit better? Oh, well. Speaking of things that make no sense…at this beer cart, only one—count 'em—*one* item is actually from Norway, a beer called Aass Pilsner. (Too easy.) The other ales are from Iceland. If you're doing the famous "drinking around the world" tour, you'll find that Norway is one of the weakest spots.

Kringla Bakeri og Kafe

DDP: One credit (Q) / Cost: $
TYPE: Norwegian; Quick Service; Snacks, Lunch, and Dinner

Look for the hanging pretzel that denotes the entrance. This quick-service location is home to one of the most famous Epcot treats, school bread, a sweet cardamom bun filled with vanilla crème custard and topped with glazed and toasted coconuts. Other sweet treats include the troll horn (cloudberry jam with whipped cream in a crispy pastry sugar-coated shell). That's not even the tip of the iceberg with desserts at Kringla. This is a must-do for anyone with a sweet tooth.

If you're looking for more savory options, you can get a ham and apple sandwich, Norwegian meatballs served with mashed potatoes and gravy (either alone or as part of a combo), a smoked pastrami salmon sandwich, or a Norwegian chef salad. An Uncrustable is the Disney Check meal.

You might fare better here than at the beer cart if you're drinking around the world. They have a Linie Aquavit (similar to vodka, but not vodka) glacier shot and draft beer from Scandinavia.

Akershus Royal Banquet Hall
DDP: One credit (T) / Cost: $$$ (TiW)
TYPE: Norwegian; Character Buffet; Breakfast, Lunch, and Dinner
This is one of those breakfast exceptions in the World Showcase. Breakfast is bustling at Akershus because...princesses. This may be a cheaper (see: only one DDP credit) and easier-to-get reservation than Cinderella's Royal Table if you have someone in your party that's just gotta meet the princesses. Even though it's not in *the* medieval castle, it's in *a* medieval castle. You'll find some combination of Snow White, Cinderella, Belle, Princess Aurora, and Ariel here. If you time your breakfast reservation right, you might be able to meet Anna and Elsa, too (with minimal wait)—in their hugely popular ride—Frozen Ever After, right next to Akershus.

For breakfast, it's all-you-care-to-enjoy eggs, bacon, sausage and potato casserole. There's a buffet with non-breakfast items like salami, pork loin, turkey, salmon, cheese, and garnishes. Breakfast costs $49 for adults and $26.99 for kids. Lunch and dinner are the same menu and same price: $60.71 for adults and $36.21 for children. Each begins with a "Taste of Norway" complete with seafoods, meats, cheeses, salad, and fruit. Then, you choose from one of the rotating entrées: Norwegian meatballs, seared pork, salmon, potato dumplings, stuffed pasta, or chicken breast. You end your meal with an assortment of traditional Norwegian desserts. Disney Check meals are salmon, grilled chicken breast, and beef medallions. Other kids' meals are mac and cheese, pizza, and Norwegian meatballs. There are quite a few specialty cocktails for adults and many wines from which to choose.

World Showcase: China

China Kiosks, Wagons, and Carts

The Joy of Tea is located along the World Showcase Lagoon and is much more than that. You'll find tea, ginger and strawberry red bean ice cream, smoothies, cocktails, and snacks. You can opt for the Lucky Combo, a curry chicken pocket, two egg rolls, a soft drink, and ice cream. For $10.98, this would be considered a Disney deal, and it would probably be your China stop if you were drinking around the world. Try the Tipsy Ducks in Love if you need a boost of energy: bourbon whisky, coffee, black tea, cream, and chocolate syrup. For those who like fruity cocktails, try the Canto Loopy: vodka and cantaloupe juice.

Lotus Blossom Café

DDP: One credit (Q) / Cost: $
TYPE: Chinese; Quick Service; Snacks, Lunch, and Dinner

You'll find lots of your favorite Chinese dishes here: Mongolian-style beef noodles, veggie stir fry, Sichuan spicy chicken, sesame chicken salad, shrimp fried rice, and orange chicken. You can also get egg rolls and potstickers if you're looking for something light. There's nothing supremely unique about this location, but the food is serviceable. I'm a fan of going here for just a snack (potstickers when it's not the Food and Wine Festival) to keep my energy levels up during the day.

Nine Dragons Restaurant

DDP: One credit (T) / Cost: $$ (TiW)
TYPE: Chinese; Unique/Themed; Lunch and Dinner

A few years ago, I was planning a WDW trip with a group of friends. We were talking about planning our ADRs, and I suggested Nine Dragons. A few of my friends scoffed at me, "Katherine, we can get Chinese food at home, why would we go to Disney World for it?" Boy, were they eating their words! Nine Dragons is what I would classify as a hidden gem. It's not widely known as a restaurant where you *must* eat on your vacation, but it is consistent, delicious, and the service is great.

The lunch and dinner menus vary a bit. For lunch, you can get the Nine Dragons Lunch Box, which consists of Kowloon Spare

Ribs, General Tso's Chicken Bao Bun, and choice of soup. This is a great option to sample a few items on the menu, and I highly recommend the General Tso's Bao Buns as they are delicious little clouds of spicy chicken. Other lunch entrées are Happy Family (stir-fried beef, shrimp, chicken, and veggies), Moo Goo Gai Pan (stir-fried chicken, snow peas, carrots, mushrooms), Kung Pao Chicken or Shrimp, Typhoon Shelter Shrimp (fried shrimp with shallots, garlic, jalapeños, and sweet chili aioli), Five-spiced Fish, Veggie and Tofu Stir Fry, Grandma's Pork Belly, Canton Pepper Beef, Honey-Sesame Chicken, Nine Dragons Fried Rice, and Roast Duck Salad. The dessert items are banana cheesecake egg rolls (this serves two), ice cream (strawberry-red ben or caramel-ginger flavor), or Chinese ginger cake. There are no Disney Check meals; instead, kids can choose from Honey Chicken, Kid's Deluxe entrée with shrimp and chicken with sweet and sour sauce, egg-fried rice, carrots and broccoli, and lastly, sweet and sour shrimp with lo mein. Nine Dragons offers many specialty cocktails that you won't find anywhere else in Epcot, like the Ginger Zinger (ginger liqueur, light rum, ginger ale, with a lemon twist), Shanghai Fusion (light rum, cherry brandy, plum wine, grapefruit and pineapple juices), and Heavenly Clouds (coconut rum, honeydew melon liqueur, pineapple juice, cream float). There are also several non-alcoholic specialties, like the strawberry smoothie, Shangri-La Smoothie (exotically fruity and tangy fusion of strawberry and mango), iced chai tea, and the Hainan Sunrise (orange juice, seltzer, with a hint of mango). At Nine Dragons, even the beverage menu is extensive if you want to order something other than a Coke, such as blackberry jasmine iced tea or jasmine tea.

At dinner, you can opt for the same entrée choices as lunch, but they've added grilled lamb chops with a garlic-cumin glaze, sweet-and-sour vegetables, and coconut sticky rice. Most notably, you can get the Nine Dragons Family Dinner after 4:30 p.m. It affords you the choice of one soup (hot and sour or chicken dumpling consommé), one entrée (honey sesame chicken, Canton pepper beef, or Grandma's pork belly) and one dessert (either of the ice cream flavors).

The atmosphere at Nine Dragons is tranquil and relaxing. I've never been in there when it's been loud. You can request a table by the windows for prime-time people watching. Overall, this restaurant is fairly priced for what you get. If you're typically a family who eats on-the-go in Disney World and doesn't like to commit to sit-down meals, this is the perfect place to dip your toe—good food at an affordable price with quick service. And no, it's not the same Chinese food you can get at home.

World Showcase: Germany

Germany Kiosks, Wagons, and Carts

Since we are travelling from China to Germany, it's only fair that I mention the Refreshment Outpost. As you cross the bridge from China, you'll see what looks like a small African village. Geographically, this makes no sense, but hey, we're in Epcot, so throw that logic away! The Refreshment Outpost serves hot dogs, ice cream treats, and beverages of both the alcoholic and non-alcoholic persuasion. In Germany proper, be sure to wander into the Weinkeller, a small wine shop serving German wine by the flights and by the glass. The world-famous Bier Stand sells, you guessed it, beer and pretzels—but not the Mickey kind with the goopy fake cheese. This is a real German pretzel. One of the most sought-after beers is the Schofferhofer grapefruit beer. The Bier Stand used to be one of the only places in WDW to serve it, but Disney knows how popular it is and so you will see it popping up in other locations, even in other parks. The line is usually pretty long for the Bier Stand, but another option close by for German brews is the Trinken Cart right on the promenade. Interestingly enough, the Trinken Cart has *more* options than the Bier Stand, and you can get the (real German) pretzel there, too. Vacation, hacked.

Karamell-Kuche

DDP: One credit (S) / Cost: $
TYPE: German/American; Quick service; Snacks

This ain't your Grandma's candy. Well, actually it is. You know those delightful Werther's Originals that grandmas worldwide seem to have at their immediate disposal? Imagine a whole store of Werther's treats. The shop itself looks like a small Bavarian home, and Karamell-Kuche is truly one of my favorite spots for souvenirs. They have tons of food that's easy to pack and the treats are unique enough for the folks back home. Just be sure to get some for yourself, too. My favorite is the made-in-store caramel corn. It's so good—especially if you let it get a little warm in your backpack. If caramel isn't your thing, they have a ton of other candies and chocolates, too. Try the hand-dipped chocolate pineapple spear, or another of my favorites, the chocolate marshmallow. Stop inside Karamell-Kuche to beat the heat and watch the cast members make the candy!

Sommerfest

DDP: One credit (Q) / Cost: $
TYPE: German; Quick service; Snacks, Lunch, and Dinner

Grab a bratwurst or frankfurter at this counter service spot in the back of the Germany Pavilion. You can get a German pretzel, nudel gratin, and macaroni salad as sides. For dessert, there is an apple strudel with vanilla sauce as well as Black Forest cake. You can also sample a different variety of beers here compared to the Bier Stand and the Trinken Cart. I think this location is often forgotten because it is tucked away near the entrance to the table-service Biergarten. There are indoor tables (in air conditioning) designated as seating for Sommerfest. You will also find seating outside.

Biergarten

DDP: One credit (T) / Cost: $$-$$$ (TiW)
TYPE: German; Unique/Themed; Lunch and Dinner

Transport yourself to an Oktoberfest celebration and indulge in a "Boisterous German Buffet" at Biergarten. You'll be treated to live entertainment, dancing, and plenty of beer drinking if you choose to dine here. I hope you aren't shy about making new friends, because depending on your group's size, you'll be seated with other families. Even for lunch, the atmosphere is dark (a la the Mexico Pavilion) and is meant to look like twilight in a Bavarian village. You'll be surrounded by trees and gurgling fountains. There's a stage and a dance floor where German performers will ring bells and polka their way into your hearts. This is one of the places where you'll see a price difference in lunch and dinner. Lunch costs $33 for adults, $18 for children. Dinner costs $40 for adults, $22 for children.

The buffet offerings are nearly the same for lunch and dinner. The only difference is that for lunch, frikadellen is on the menu. What's frikadellen? They are Germany's answer to hamburgers. At dinner time, frikadellen is removed from the menu and replaced with sauerbraten—German pot roast. Otherwise, you can find salads, a carving station, braised red cabbage, potatoes, schnitzel, sausages, rotisserie chicken, roasted salmon, sauerkraut, spaetzle (soft egg noodle), and assorted desserts on both menus.

If German food and beer is your cup of tea, Biergarten is a fun time. Even if German food and beer is not your cup of tea, Biergarten is a fun time—as well as a waste of $40 because you won't be enjoying the food. Like a lot of the Disney buffets, the focus of this place is the atmosphere-slash-experience and not the food. If you're looking for first-rate food, go elsewhere.

World Showcase: Italy

Italy Kiosks, Wagons, and Carts

Get a refreshing gelato-to-go at the Gelati kiosk. Cannolis (in classic and cupcake form) and tiramisu can be ordered here as well. The donkey cart, back by the entrance to Via Napoli, serves a tiramisu popsicle, lemon sorbet, and spumone gelato cup. You can also purchase limoncello/orangecello cocktails there, as well as Italian wines. Speaking of Italian wines, step into Enoteca Castello, where you can taste wines by the glass or try a flight. If you're in a rush, and are in the mood for pizza, to the left of the entrance to Via Napoli you'll see a walk-up counter (Pizza al Taglio) with a small selection of pizzas and wines. The pizza here is not the same as that served in Via Napoli; it's thicker and square in shape.

Tutto Gusto Wine Cellar

DDP: No / Cost: $
TYPE: Italian; Lounge; Snacks, Lunch, and Dinner

Mexico has the San Angels, and Italy has the Tuttos. This hideaway is in the back-left corner of the Italy Pavilion. At the door, you will see a host stand and you will find something most unusual—the inability to make dining reservations! This is amazing, because Tutto Gusto is the kind of place where you'll want to take a spontaneous respite from the heat. The wine cellar is dark, cozy, and intimate—you can sit comfortably on couches or at small tables. It is not ideal for big groups.

If you had your heart set on Tutto Italia Ristorante, the sit-down restaurant next door, and you weren't able to get a reservation, you can order off their menu here. You can also order a customized selection of meats and cheeses. There are paninis and delicious Italian-style desserts. The wine list is impressive, because, well, it's a wine cellar. My favorite is the sangria—it comes in a *big* pitcher—which ends up being a pretty good deal for the amount of drink you get. I always intend on just stopping by Tutto Gusto Wine Cellar and end up hanging out longer than I anticipate because the atmosphere is so cozy.

Tutto Italia Ristorante
DDP: One credit (T) / Cost: $$$ (TiW)
TYPE: Italian; Unique/Themed; Lunch and Dinner

Tutto Italia resembles a large restaurant you'd find in Rome. The walls are adorned with murals, and the dining room is typically full and loud as chandeliers hang overhead. There is a side dining room which overlooks the pavilion's piazza, but (most importantly) it is still inside the air conditioning.

The dinner menu is a bit more extensive (and expensive) than the lunch menu. Classic Italian dishes on the menu include ravioli, spaghetti, lasagna, chicken, salmon, veal, pork chop, and lamb chop. For lunch, a lot of the meat options are cut in favor of lighter fare like paninis.

Kids can order spaghetti, mozzarella sticks, pan-seared pizza, and chicken tenders for lunch or dinner. There are no Disney Check meals. End your meal with desserts like panna cotta, tiramisu, bacio al cioccolato (warm hazelnut chocolate cake, vanilla gelato with chocolate sauce), cannoli, lemon ricotta cheesecake, and assorted gelato.

Adults can order a plethora of Italian wines, a choice of several beers, and specialty cocktails, from espresso martinis to peach bellinis.

Tutto Italia Ristorante has always been the big, flashy, popular Italian restaurant in Epcot. It has a romantic, classic setting. However, as far as the food goes, it's nothing special, which is unfortunate for me because Italian food is my favorite. If you're going to eat in Italy, I would suggest heading over to Via Napoli Ristoranti e Pizzeria instead.

Via Napoli Ristoranti e Pizzeria

DDP: One credit (T) / Cost: $$-$$$ (TiW)
TYPE: Italian; Unique/Themed; Lunch and Dinner

Step into the very back of the Italy Pavilion to find Via Napoli. While Tutto Italia has more of a classic, Roman inspiration, Via Napoli samples the best of southern Italy—mainly, pizza. The atmosphere is more relaxed and less formal than Tutto Gusto, with high ceilings and tables that are rather close together. If you order a pizza at Via Napoli it will be cooked in one the wood-burning ovens named for famous Italian volcanoes: Stromboli, Etna, or Vesuvius. I find this restaurant to be a better overall experience than some of the other places in the Italy Pavilion, because it lends itself to sharing: pizza, appetizers, and desserts.

The same menu is for both lunch and dinner. Start with one of the antipasti (small plates) to share. You can order Vongole "Oreganata" for either two or five which consists of clams, bread crumbs, oregano, pancetta, and lemon; caponata (crostino, eggplant, pine nuts, celery, onions, and red pepper), calamari fritti (fried calamari), crochette di patate (fried potato and ham fritter), scampi (shrimp in garlic and butter), arancini (fried risotto balls), mozzarella caprese (with tomatoes and basil), cimarola (fried stuffed artichokes, taleggio, and prosciutto); and antipasto misto (chef's selection of cured meats, cheese, assorted salads and vegetables) which serves 2–3 people. There are plenty of soups and salads. You can also order traditional Italian pasta dishes like fettuccini, lasagna, and spaghetti.

However, the keystone of this menu is the pizza. Via Napoli is arguably the best pizza on property. You can choose from traditional options like margherita with tomato, mozzarella and basil, or pepperoni with cheese and tomato sauce. There are more adventurous options, like Prosciutto e Melone (white pizza with fontina, mozzarella, prosciutto, cantaloupe, and arugula). Or, try the Affumicata (white pizza with mozzarella, smoked salmon, arugula, pomodorini, and stracchino). My favorite lies somewhere in between the classic and the adventurous—the broccolini pizza with cherry tomatoes, mozzarella, porchetta, robiola, and broccolini. Pizzas here come in three sizes: individual, large (serves 2–3), and mezzo metro (serves 3–5). I also like to add the family-style house salad to my pizza that comes with mixed greens, cucumber, pepperoncini peppers, peppadew peppers, diced tomatoes, and olives, in a red wine vinaigrette. This costs $7 per person as long as at least two people order it. Kids can choose from margherita pizza, breaded and fried mozzarella bites, and spaghetti and meatballs.

To cap off your meal, there are several dessert options, including gelato, tiramisu, cannolis, "ugly but good" amarena cherry and vanilla gelato sundae, ice cream soda made with gelato, Zeppola di Caterina (ricotta cheese fritters served with whipped cream and chocolate sauce), and Torta Caprese (a traditional Neopolitan chocolate-hazelnut and almond cake). There are a few beers on the menu and also some signature cocktails. If you're a fan of the Moscow Mule, try the Limoncello Mule: Grey Goose l'orange vodka, limoncello, peach puree, orange juice, pineapple juice, lime juice, and ginger beer—served in a copper mug, of course. It's super refreshing on a hot day.

The only knock I have on Via Napoli is that sometimes the service can be slow. Not bad, but slow. I've always found the servers to be attentive and kind. This is one of my all-time-favorites—not only in Epcot but in all of Walt Disney World.

World Showcase: The American Adventure

American Adventure Kiosks, Wagons, and Carts

You'll find the standard frozen treats available for purchase in America, as well as a Joffrey's location with coffee and pastries. Wet your whistle at Block and Hans. Disney describes this kiosk as a place where "Purveyors of Fine American Ale" introduce you to some of the great craft beers. Block and Hans has a rotating selection of beers—this is usually my spot to drink in America, and by press time it ought to have a new draft system in place, for beers on tap. I really like the Killer Whale Cream Ale by Bold City Brewery. Fife and Drum Tavern is another spot in America to get more traditional American brews, such as Sam Adams, Bud Light, and Yuengling. Fife and Drum has turkey legs, soft-serve ice cream, and popcorn, too. You'll probably smell the funnel cake stand next to Block and Hans before you see it. The stand sells funnel cakes and ice cream in any combination thereof.

Liberty Inn

DDP: One credit (Q) / Cost: $
TYPE: American; Quick Service; Lunch and Dinner

My country tis of thee, sweet land of nuggets, burgers, and fries. As a kid, I'm sure this was the only place in Epcot where I'd eat. I'd like to go on the record and apologize to my parents for making them eat here when they had far better choices available. Don't eat here. Seriously. In addition to nuggets, burgers, and fries, this large cafeteria-style eatery serves up fried chicken, hot dogs, pork barbeque, fried shrimp, and Cobb salads. You can mobile order, but you still have to walk into Liberty Inn to pick up your food, so you aren't completely escaping the judgment of surrounding tourists. It's a shame that America doesn't have better food options. I mean, c'mon, you're on the home turf here! Even the pavilion is called the American Adventure. This isn't plain old Canada or Mexico, America is an *adventure*—but, sadly, the food is not. I will give America an honorable mention during festival time as they usually have pretty good food and drink offerings at their kiosks , but other than that, there's nothing worthy of your taste buds.

World Showcase: Japan

Japan Kiosks, Wagons, and Carts

Kabuki Café will be one of the first places you pass traveling from America to Japan, and it's worth making a stop. Come for the sushi, stay for the shaved ice. Japanese shaved ice, also known as Kakigōri, is on the menu for kids and adults. If you're over 21, try a sake mist—alcoholic shaved ice in blood orange, coconut pineapple, or blackberry flavors. They also have a variety of Japanese beers, sakes, and plum wine. If you decide on ordering a Kirin beer, you can get it frozen, which is essentially a beer slushy. The Japan Beverage Stand toward the back of the pavilion also sells Japanese beers, specialty drinks, sake, and wine. Also, if you wander all the way to the back of the large gift shop found in the Japan pavilion, Mitsukoshi, you'll find a bar completely dedicated to sake. This is a fun, crowded experience where people cheer you on while downing shots of sake. This is exactly why Epcot is my favorite park!

Katsura Grill
DDP: One credit (Q) / Cost: $
TYPE: Japanese; Quick Service; Snacks, Lunch, and Dinner
Located a few steps above the World Showcase Promenade, surrounded by a koi garden, the Katsura grill brings zen to the quick-service meal. Here you'll find popular sushi like California rolls, a combo with nigiri, spicy rolls, and vegetable rolls. Their noodle menu includes Shrimp Tempura Udon, Spicy Seafood Miso Ramen, Beef Udon, and Tonkotsu Ramen (served with pork and vegetables). They also have shrimp and chicken teriyaki, chicken and beef teriyaki, and chicken cutlet curry. Kids can order chicken, chicken and shrimp, or beef and shrimp teriyakis. You can order fountain beverages, teas, as well as Japanese beer and wine to add to your meal. There is indoor seating available with lots of natural light. Even though the space is relatively small, large tables with bench seating makes it optimal for larger parties. You can also eat outside in the koi garden.

Teppan Edo
DDP: One credit (T) / Cost: $$
TYPE: Japanese; Unique/Themed; Lunch and Dinner
Climb the stairs above Mitsukoshi to find both of the Japanese table-service options. Facing the World Showcase Lagoon is Tokyo Dining; in the back, Teppan Edo. Teppan Edo is a hibachi restaurant where you may be seated with other guests to fill your table. You'll watch your chef cook your food right before your eyes. The meals are fun, and the chefs try to get everyone

involved in the experience. Before you get to the grill, you can try sushi, ribs, soup, assorted tempura, and edamame as appetizers. For entrées, pick between the following proteins: filet mignon, julienne beef (served with udon noodles), ebi (grilled shrimp with udon noodles), hotate (cold-water ocean scallops with udon noodles), NY cut steak, salmon, tori (chicken with udon noodles), and yasai (seasonal vegetables and tofu). You can also choose combinations of steak and shrimp, chicken and shrimp, and steak and chicken. You can pay out of pocket for add-ons like Wagyu steak, tuna tataki, mushrooms, brown rice, lobster tail, sea scallop, chicken breast, shrimp, and asparagus. Kids can choose from chicken, shrimp, and steak for their entrées. A variety of mousse cakes and ice cream is available for dessert. There are many specialty drinks, as well as sake, beer, and wine.

Now, let's talk about the value of Teppan Edo. I like Teppan Edo. I really do. I spent my 30th birthday with a group of 25 of my friends in one of those small rooms catching zucchini in my mouth and oohing and ahhing over an onion volcano. But, I could do that at home, too. Teppan Edo is a fairly standard hibachi restaurant. What makes it different from your local hibachi restaurant is the price. You are very aware that you are paying the Disney premium here. Take that into consideration while planning your ADRs.

Tokyo Dining

DDP: One credit (T) / Cost: $$ (TiW)
TYPE: Japanese; Unique/Themed; Lunch and Dinner
Where Teppan Edo is the more rowdy and louder environment, think of Tokyo Dining as the classier take on Japanese fare in Epcot. It is co-located with Teppan Edo, but faces the front of the building. Time your reservation right and ask for a seat by the window for a good view of IllumiNations. The restaurant is made to look like an establishment you'd find in Tokyo, complete with mood lighting and napkins of origami art.

The lunch and dinner menus are identical, price and content, and the menu is extensive. Begin your meal with edamame, panko-crusted shrimp, spicy calamari tempura, miso soup (of both veggie and clam varieties), seafood yuzu shio ramen (ramen noodles with grilled shrimp and asari claim in yuzu-seafood broth), garden salad, or tuna-salmon-poke salad. You'll find a variety of sashimi and nigiri here, too. Specialty sushi rolls include a spicy crunchy roll (tuna and salmon topped with tempura crunch, dynamite and volcano drizzle), California roll (crab meat, avocado, cucumber, smelt roe, and Japanese mayo), vegetable roll (cucumber, kanpyo, asparagus, pickled ginger, and carrot topped with avocado and sesame seeds), volcano roll (grilled California roll topped with shrimp, scallops, and volcano sauce), firecracker roll (tempura shrimp roll with wakame salad and jalapeño finished with eel sauce, shredded red pepper, and sriracha drizzle), and the dragon monster roll (avocado, cucumber, cream cheese topped with eel, smelt roe, micro green, and dynamite sauce). You can also order salmon, grilled chicken, filet mignon, and rack of lamb. If you just can't decide, try the Chef's Creation Bento Box. It consists of shrimp and vegetable tempura, New York sirloin steak with garlic-ginger sauce, chicken teriyaki, tuna-salmon-poke salad with sesame-ginger dressing, tuna roll, salmon roll, shrimp nigiri roll, and a vegetable roll. Children can get chicken tempura nuggets or a California roll. There are many specialty alcoholic beverages that range from rum to sake-based drinks. You can order wine, sake, and beer. Try the premium beer tasting with Asahi Super Dry, Sapporo Black, and Kirin lager, paired with edamame. Teppan Edo and Tokyo Dining share the same dessert menu. It consists of green tea mousse cake, mango mousse cake, ginger mousse cake, and soft-serve ice cream (green tea, vanilla, or green tea and vanilla swirl).

World Showcase: Morocco

Morocco Kiosks, Wagons, and Carts

You can find coffees, pastries and frozen drinks at the stands in Morocco. At the Spice Road Table Juice Bar, there are wines, beers, and alcoholic or non-alcoholic slushies. This is my idea of a juice bar—no juice, lots of alcohol.

Tangierine Café

DDP: One credit (Q) / Cost: $
TYPE: Moroccan; Quick Service; Snacks, Lunch and Dinner

While the kid's meals are simple nuggets and burgers, the adult menu at Tangierine Café samples the best of the Mediterranean. There is a shawarma chicken platter, a shawarma lamb platter, and a combo platter that includes both. You'll also find a vegetable platter, Moroccan kefta platter, and saffron rotisserie chicken. You can order tabouleh, marinated olives, lentil salad, and Tangierine couscous salad as sides.

You may have gotten the impression (see my Liberty Inn writeup) that I am a picky eater. I proudly call myself a reformed picky eater, and I want to tell you a tale of the first time I ate at Tangierine Café. I was visiting Epcot with some friends from college, and this was my first time in Disney as an adult without my parents. It was time for lunch and my friends suggested we eat at Tangierine Café. My knees buckled, and my palms got a little sweaty and the picky eater in me was about to say, "I'll catch you guys later..."—cut to me laying in the fetal position under a table at Liberty Inn crying into a tray of nuggets and fries. I resisted this urge. I walked bravely into Tangierine Café and ordered the shawarma chicken platter, which is essentially just grilled chicken and not all that exotic, but guys, I did it. The lesson to be learned here is if you've been to Disney a few times, and you always find yourself going back to your old faithful spots, be open to trying something new. You might just impress yourself!

Restaurant Marrakesh

DDP: One credit (T) / Cost: $$ (TiW)
TYPE: Moroccan; Unique/Themed; Lunch and Dinner

Surround yourself with beautiful Moroccan architecture, music, and belly dancers. Yes, the belly dancers here are modest and family-friendly. We are in Disney World, after all. This extensive menu boasts Moroccan specialties like lemon chicken tagine (braised half chicken with garlic, green olives, and preserved ham), couscous with vegetables (the food so nice they named it twice), chicken kebabs, braised beef short ribs "Meshoui-style" (garlic aged butter and cumin salt, roasted garlic mashed potatoes, and baby carrots), shrimp chermoula tangine (artichoke bottoms, pearl onions, small potatoes, and saffron-anise broth), Mogador grouper tangine (marinated with olives, lemon confit, potatoes, green pepper, and chermoula), beef tenderloin shish kebab, roasted lamb shank, pan-seared lamb loin medallions with hummus-rosemary pancakes, and North Atlantic salmon (OK, not from Morocco). While kids can get nuggets (of both the chicken and fish persuasion), burgers, and fries, they can also order beef-kebabs and Moroccan-style pasta.

For dinner, you can try the Taste of Morocco. It includes Moroccan salads, choice of beef tenderloin shish kebab with chicken brochettes, Merguez sausage, and braised lamb or couscous and seven vegetables served with steamed semolina pasta and finished with assorted baklava. There are many appetizers that cater to sharing with your party. A few specialty drinks round off the menu.

Restaurant Marrakesh is a good choice if you want to eat in the World Showcase but didn't plan ahead. It's easy to get reservations here. I just did a quick, unofficial, science experiment and tried to get a reservation for two for the night I'm writing this, and there were plenty available.

Spice Road Table
DDP: One credit (T) / Cost: $$ (TiW)
TYPE: Moroccan; Unique/Themed; Lunch and Dinner

Even though Restaurant Marrakesh has the flashy belly dancers and extensive menu, Spice Road Table is my favorite Moroccan eatery. It is right on the World Showcase Lagoon and is a great place for IllumiNations viewing—ask for a table by the water. They do take reservations, but I've found that there's often availability if you just walk up and ask. It doesn't hurt to try.

While Spice Road Table does have plenty of traditional, full-size entrées, like roasted chicken, NY strip steak, and rack of lamb, it's their small plates that have my heart. Mostly, the brie fondue—warm, melty cheese with baguettes. You just can't go wrong! I also really like the hummus and olive dish. The beer, wine, and signature drink listing is more impressive here than anywhere else in the Morocco Pavilion. This is a great spot to stop, smell the roses, and have a drink.

World Showcase: France

Kiosks, Wagons, and Carts

It just feels wrong not to be holding a baguette and drinking a glass of wine while walking through France. For the wine part, head to Les Vins des Chefs de France. This kiosk on the water has plenty of reds, whites, and other premium wines. You can also order champagne or Kronenbourg 1664 (which I lovingly refer to as the Budweiser of French beers, and I mean that as a compliment). If you're in need of something refreshing with a little kick, try the Grand Marnier Orange Slush, with Grand Marnier, rum, Grey Goose Orange, and orange juice. Crepes des Chefs de France is also on the water, serving delicious crepes. You can pick from sugar, chocolate, or strawberry, and you can also get yours topped with ice cream. I say it's OK to indulge on this dessert any time—you're on vacation! I know I shouldn't talk about the festival kiosks that are open during one of Epcot's three yearly festivals, but this is important. France has the best kiosks. The drink and food options available are unmatched. They usually have Kronenbourg 1664's cooler, younger sibling Kronenbourg Blanc on tap, as well as a few delicious small plates from which to order. If you're planning your trip around a festival, be sure to stop in France.

L'Artisan des Glaces

DDP: One credit (S) / Cost: $
TYPE: French; Quick Service; Snacks

Don't overlook this small shop that seems to blend in with the other storefronts as you walk deep into the France Pavilion. L'Artisan des Glaces specializes in ice cream and sorbet, and their flavor offerings vary by the season. Spruce up your ice cream order by getting it served inside a macaron, or inside one of their homemade waffle cones or bowls. Adults can order the famous ice cream martini: two scoops of ice cream with a shot of Grand Marnier and whipped cream vodka or rum.

Les Halles Boulangerie-Patisserie

DDP: One credit (Q) / Cost: $
TYPE: French; Quick Service; Snacks, Lunch, and Dinner

At the back of the France Pavilion sits Les Halles Boulange-rie-Patisserie. This is France's quick-service location. From pastries to sandwiches, you'll find sweet and savory treats to satisfy any appetite. Nothing will make you feel more Parisian than ordering a glass of red wine and sampling a selection of cheeses with a baguette fresh from the oven. The pastry menu here is enormous, and to view all the treats under glass is like looking at works of art. You'll find macarons, tarts, crème brûlée, eclairs, and parfaits. The seating is a bit limited, but it's inside, so it's a good spot to seek shelter from Florida storms and Florida heat. They do have sandwiches, soups, and salads, but my favorite thing to do in Les Halles is to order a few things to share with my traveling companions, and then just hang out and talk. The food here is really good, so if you wanted to commit to making a full meal out of your trip here, it wouldn't be a mistake.

Les Chefs De France

DDP: One credit (T) / Cost: $$ (TiW for lunch only)
TYPE: French; Unique/Themed; Lunch and Dinner

You'll spot this restaurant by the mass of people waiting under its awning for a table. Les Chefs is designed to look like an authentic Parisian bistro. Don't let the line outside fool you— you can often walk up and get reservations. This is one of Epcot's original restaurants. It opened with the park in 1982 by French culinary notables Roger Vergé, Gaston Lenôtre, and Paul Bocuse (the namesake of Monsieur Paul—keep reading!). Paul's son Jerome manages both this restaurant and Monsieur Paul.

The menu is the same for lunch and dinner. You'll find classic French cuisine with simple ingredients. The list of appetizers includes escargot, charcuterie, French onion soup, and flatbreads. For your main course, you'll see a selection ranging from gratin de macaroni (baked macaroni) to duck breast with cherries. They also have a prix fixe menu, where you can choose soup or salad to start. Then, choose braised beef, salmon, roasted chicken, or baked macaroni for your main course, followed by a dessert selection. The children's menu is a truncated version of the main menu with similar chicken, salmon, beef, and pasta options. They do serve alcohol here, although (weirdly) Disney does not have it listed on their website. What's French food without some wine?

Les Chefs De France does not disappoint. In fact, this was a restaurant I remember having fond memories of as a child (I spent my 11th birthday lunch here), and one I kept visiting again and again as an adult. I put myself on a temporary ban of eating at Les Chefs De France because I found myself drawn to it during every trip. This helped me finally try all the other excellent restaurant options around the World Showcase. The one knock I'll give on Les Chefs is that the atmosphere is a little too loud and the quarters are a bit too close. The tables are very close together, and I always feel like I'm bumping into someone when navigating my way through the restaurant. The menu is a little bit more accessible than Monsieur Paul, so this is the more popular, bustling, sit-down restaurant in France.

Monsieur Paul

DDP: Two credits (T) / Cost: $$$
TYPE: French; Fine/Signature; Dinner

Tucked away above the hustle and bustle of Les Chefs de France is Monsieur Paul. This is one of the newer editions to the World Showcase. It was revamped and renamed in late 2012. The reason it's two dining credits is because this is truly a gourmet dining experience. The titular "Paul" is Chef Paul Bocuse, a pioneer of *nouvelle cuisine*, which stresses the importance high quality, fresh ingredients.

For dinner, you can choose your items à la carte, or you can order from one of the prix-fixe menus. The first course for the prix fixe "prestige" menu is green asparagus with veloute and lemon cream. For your second-course appetizer, you can choose from oxtail broth with braised beef, vegetables, and black winter truffles covered in puff pastry, oven-baked egg, peas salad, arugula, truffle cream, and green asparagus, or ahi tuna served three-ways: cured, seared, and in rillettes, or Niçoise-style. Your third (main) course consists of Dover sole with tagliatelles, mushrooms, and creamy sabayon, roasted lamb chop and braised saddle with vegetables and polenta apoleon, lamb jus, or roasted duck magret with white bean purée and fricassee and braised crispy duck. There is another prix-fixe menu that caters more toward sampling a bit of everything—the Prix Fixe Menu Dégustation. Kids can choose from seared chicken tenders (fancy nuggets!), grilled beef tenderloin, and roasted salmon. It wouldn't be a fancy French restaurant without fancy French desserts, including an array of meringue, ice cream, almond cake, caramelized apples, and a milk chocolate sphere.

This restaurant is more quiet, spacious, and upscale than its downstairs neighbor, Les Chefs De France. It also provides a good view of the World Showcase Lagoon. This is one of the few dining locations in Disney World that enforces a dress code. Disney requires that men wear khakis, slacks or dress shorts, and collared shirts. Sport coats are optional. Women must wear Capri pants, skirts, dresses or dress shorts. For either gender, jeans may be worn if in good condition. Not permitted are tank tops, flip-flops, swimsuits, swimsuit cover-ups, hats for gentlemen, cut-offs, torn clothing, and t-shirts with offensive language and/or graphics. Monsieur Paul also boasts a specific New Year's Eve menu if you plan on eating there during a holiday visit.

World Showcase: United Kingdom

United Kingdom Kiosks, Wagons, and Carts

Outside the Rose and Crown, you'll find a green counter that sells Bass Ale, Harp Lager, and Magners Pear Cider. You can also buy a bag of seasoned, house-made crisps (chips) to complement your drink. Yum, salt and beer.

Yorkshire County Fish Shop

DDP: One credit (Q) / Cost: $
TYPE: British; Quick Service; Snacks, Lunch, and Dinner

Yorkshire County is essentially a glorified window, only a step above a kiosk or cart *structurally*, but man, it's so good. This fact is borne out by the long line of people waiting for delicious, fried deliciousness. The main menu item and specialty is fish and chips. You can also order Victoria sponge cake with jam and buttercream, fruit, sodas, tea, coffee, Bass Ale, or Harp Lager. This is an excellent use of a quick service credit. The food is amazing, and the portion sizes are rather large. The chips you get here are not your typical Disney fries—they are thick-cut (more like steak fries). I will give Yorkshire County Fish Shop the ultimate compliment: when Epcot has their yearly festivals, and I can choose from nearly any cuisine in the entire world, I *still* sometimes opt for the fish and chips here.

Rose and Crown Pub

DDP: No / Cost: $ (TiW)
TYPE: British; Unique/Themed; Snacks, Lunch, and Dinner

This bustling British pub is always crowded and lively, but you cannot make reservations. If you grab a table, you can get waited on by a server, but you can also go directly to the bar where you'll find the bartenders are always friendly. If you order from the bar, there are a few high-top tables near the entrance where you can congregate. There are also often live musicians performing in the pub.

The limited food menu includes fish and chips, battered banger and chips, and Scotch egg and British Butty (your choice of chips, bacon, or banger on a brioche roll with crisps and house-made pickled onions). Let's face it, you aren't going to a British pub for the food. The real reason you're here is the drinks. Specialty drinks range from the Welsh Dragon (peach schnapps, melon liqueur, crème de menthe, orange juice, and pineapple juice served in a souvenir cup) to the Leaping Leprechaun (Jameson Irish Whiskey, Don Q Cristal Rum, Skyy Vodka, melon liqueur, and sweet-and-sour topped with Sprite). You can order a pint or a sampler of their beers on tap: Boddingtons English Pub Ale, Bass Ale, Guinness Stout, Harp Lager, Strongbow Cider, or Smithwick's. They specialize in pub blends here, mixing your favorite drinks to potentially create your *new* favorite drink—like Harp and Guinness, Sprite and Bass Ale, or my favorite, the cider and black (cider with a shot of black currant juice). The possibilities are nearly endless.

Rose and Crown Dining Room

DDP: One credit (T) / Cost: $$ (TiW)
TYPE: British; Unique/Themed; Lunch and Dinner

The Rose and Crown Dining Room gets more crowded as the day grows long. It's one of the most affordable restaurants that also has a view of IllumiNations. You'll find typical British fare on the menu, and the menu for the dining room is more extensive than the menu in the pub. You can order entrées like fish and chips, shepherd's pie, chicken masala curry, bangers and mash, corned beef and cabbage, and pan-roasted Scottish salmon. Add mushy peas or bubble and squeak as sides. The Disney Check meals are turkey flatbreads, turkey meatballs, and butter chicken. Kids can also order fish and chips, bangers and mash, and cheesy pasta. For dessert, there's sticky toffee pudding, lemon scone, chocolate nougat bar, or English trifle.

This isn't one of my favorites in Epcot. You can get the same quality fish and chips for literally half the price at Yorkshire County Fish Shop. And, if it's the energetic feeling of British culture you're craving, just stay on the pub side. If you are dying to burn a table-service credit (there's probably availability here), then go for it. But if it's the air conditioning that you're after, just grab an order of fish and chips from Yorkshire, bring it into one of the tables at the Rose and Crown Pub, and order a drink. Cheerio, chap!

World Showcase: Canada

Canada Kiosks, Wagons, and Carts

A popcorn and beer cart is located to the left of the entrance to Le Cellier Steakhouse. You can order popcorn in butter and maple varieties. They also have a few beers on tap: Moosehead, Labatt, and my favorite, Le Fin du Monde. This is one of my go-to spots in Epcot. I never really associated Canada with beer, but I'm drawn to this stand every time I'm in Epcot. If you want a different variety of drinks (beer), head up the steps to Trading Post Refreshments, a small counter attached to the inside of the Canadian gift shop. Disney touts this as a "bar," but I think you have to have at least one seat to be classified as a bar, so here it is with the kiosks, wagons, and carts. You can order Molson and Blanche de Chambly here. Blanche de Chambly is another one of my favorites, and it's from the same brewery that makes Le Fin du Monde, Unibroue. Blanche de Chambly is a Belgian-style wheat beer, the first of its kind to be bottled and marketed in North America. It's also really bubbly, so it's champagne adjacent.

Le Cellier Steakhouse

DDP: Two credits (T) / Cost: $$$ (TiW)
TYPE: Canadian; Fine/Signature; Lunch and Dinner

Settle in happy reader—it's about to get good. I could write a whole book about this place. Le Cellier is my favorite restaurant in Walt Disney World.

Le Cellier is at the base of the Canada Pavilion. You'll see a little archway with its name leading you down a flower-lined path to the door. Le Cellier is dark, and since it's at the bottom of the "Hotel de Canada" (designed to look like Canada's Château Laurier Hotel in Ottawa), it's meant to be the wine cellar. You must have a reservation to dine here. This is not one of those that restaurants that people don't know about or has a lot of capacity for walk-ins. It is one of the most highly sought-after reservations on Disney property next to Be Our Guest and Cinderella's Royal Table. If you spend any amount of time sitting in the lobby, you'll see the flotsam of sad tourists being turned away due to lack of a reservation. I will tell you, however, that cancellations *do* happen—especially if you have a party of 1–4. With a little luck, you might be able to get a same-day reservation, if you are stalking the My Disney Experience App. Just now, I searched for a dinner reservation for two on the day I'm writing this, and there was availability for an 8:45 P.M. reservation. You'd be missing IllumiNations with this reservation time, and there's no fireworks viewing in Le Cellier (you're in a cellar), but you don't need fireworks when you have a meal like this.

I first ate here in 2010. I was with my mom and my boyfriend (now husband). We were first-timers on the Disney Dining Plan. While I was certainly a fan of Disney, I was not nearly the fanatic I am today. In fact, I think I let my mom choose most of the dining experiences for that trip. I didn't know the reputation this restaurant had for being amazing, but I believed it to be warranted after I had my meal there. Back then, it was only one dining credit on the DDP. You'll see that the lunch and dinner menus are the same for price and content. Each area in the restaurant corresponds to a province or territory of Canada. When your host seats you, you'll get a brief Canadian history lesson on your province/territory. I've eaten at Le Cellier many times since 2010, and the service has always been fabulous. Is it a stereotype if it's nice? Canadians are nice people.

You'll get another Canadian history lesson when the bread basket comes out. You have a few options: sourdough, multi-grain, and a pretzel breadstick. The server will tell you how each bread option represents an area of Canada, but at this point I'm pretty much reaching my hand across the table making sure I get one of those delicious pretzel breadsticks.

The keystone of Le Cellier is the steak. Rib-eye, New York Strip, filet mignon, and a porterhouse for two ($119!) are all on the menu. If you aren't into red meat, you can also get chicken, pasta and salmon. I always get the filet here. It's AAA Canadian tenderloin served over a mushroom risotto, asparagus-tomato relish, and truffle-butter sauce. The risotto is fluffy, and the steak is always cooked to perfection.

My eyes are bigger than my stomach here, and because everything is so delicious, you'll want to try it all. Be careful, because the impending food coma is real. The sides—or enhancements, as they are called on the menu—are served family-style, so consult with your party and choose something to share. The lobster mac and cheese and loaded mashed potatoes are great. If you're looking for something more authentically Canadian to share, consider the poutine. Poutine is a Canadian dish that consists of French fries, cheese curds, and brown gravy. Yeah...not super healthy. Le Cellier often changes their menu to feature seasonal poutines. A word of warning—don't get too attached. They had a French onion poutine a few years ago, and they've since taken it off the menu. It was truly delicious. R.I.P.

They also have a prix-fixe menu, and although it might be more reasonable than ordering off the regular menu, I wouldn't recommend it because the steak options are limited. And hey, if you're eating at Le Cellier, you already know you're dropping some serious cash. So just treat yourself. Disney Check meals are grilled chicken, Mickey pasta, and seared salmon. Kids can also order Mickey mac and cheese, a grilled cheese sandwich, or a grilled strip steak.

Desserts include maple crème brûlée, warm pecan-brown butter tart, chocolate maple Yukon bar, strawberry cheesecake, and chocolate mousse maple leaf (no sugar added). The menu also includes a variety of wines, cocktails, and beers. I'm boring and usually order one of the two beers I mentioned in the kiosks, wagons, and carts section: Le Fin du Monde or Blanche de Chambly. They just pair so well with the pretzel bread. (If you don't want to stuff yourself on pretzel bread and you're *real* nice to your server, they might give you a box to take some home. Day-old pretzel bread over Mickey waffles any day.)

When I started writing this book, I polled my friends and family to gain inspiration about Disney dining. I asked them for their favorite restaurants, restaurants they've never tried but would want to, and the best dining experiences they've ever had at WDW. I asked mostly my friends who are fans of Disney, and then I asked my dad. My dad doesn't understand my adoration for Disney and pretty much rolls his eyes when I talk about it. When I asked him what his favorite Disney meal he ever had was, he said without a doubt, "that steak at Le Cellier." Make this reservation—you won't be disappointed.

CHAPTER FOUR

Disney's Hollywood Studios

Disney's Hollywood Studios was third in line to open after Magic Kingdom and Epcot, in May 1989. The park has morphed over the years from being a working studio, to developing a bigger focus on shows rather than rides. Soon, it will become the definitive Disney park for Star Wars. Unlike Magic Kingdom and Epcot, Hollywood Studios, or DHS, does not have the traditional hub-and-spoke or circular park outline. It's broken into seven, oddly shaped, themed lands: Hollywood Boulevard, Echo Lake, Commissary Lane, Grand Avenue, Toy Story Land, Animation Courtyard, and Sunset Boulevard. Even though it's one of the smaller parks, since it's not laid out efficiently, you might get more steps on your DHS-day from walking all over the park to get from one thing to the next. Hurray for Hollywood! Let's begin.

Hollywood Boulevard

This is the Studios' answer to Main Street, U.S.A. It may not evoke the same *magical* emotions, but it's themed very well. You'll pass the vintage Hollywood storefronts and advertisements as you head toward the replica of Grauman's Chinese Theatre. As you enter the park, you'll see this park's version of Crossroads of the World—with none other than Mickey Mouse perched atop the globe. Hollywood Boulevard consists mostly of stores, but there are a few places to get treats as you enter the park. You'll pass the theme-park version of the famous Brown Derby Restaurant. You might not see any celebrities, but keep your eye out for some real characters because Hollywood Boulevard is also the parade route.

Hollywood Boulevard Kiosks, Wagons, and Carts

As you walk into park, you'll spot a Coca-Cola-sponsored kiosk with soda, chips, ice cream snacks, and slushies. Sometimes, hard-to-come-by novelty sippers (think Baby Groot and BB-8) can be found here. There's a popcorn cart near the Chinese Theatre, and by the tip board (across from the Trolley Car Café). There are several stands serving Mickey bars, frozen fruit bars, and glazed nuts. Near the Chinese theatre there is a cart where you can wet your whistle with beer and chase it with a churro.

The Trolley Car Café

DDP: One credit (Q) / Cost: $
TYPE: American; Quick Service; Snacks and Drinks; Breakfast

Let's head to DHS' Starbucks location at the cross streets of Hollywood and Sunset boulevards. You'll find lots of blended frappuccinos and espressos here. You can also order cold brew, hot coffee, tea, and refreshers. There are breakfast sandwiches in the morning and roast beef and turkey sandwiches later in the day. Disney pastries are peppered into the menu, so keep an eye out for specialty cupcakes.

The Hollywood Brown Derby

DDP: Two credits (T) / Cost: $$$ (TiW)
TYPE: American; Fine/Signature; Lunch and Dinner

This is the finest dining you'll come across in DHS. The restaurant is a replica of the Brown Derby from Hollywood's Golden Age. You'll be surrounded by celebrities...on the walls, that is. See how many famous faces you can spot on the caricature-covered walls.

The original Hollywood Brown Derby was famous for its invenion of the Cobb salad. The Disney World version also has the famous Cobb salad, with finely chopped greens, turkey breast, bacon, egg, tomatoes, crumbled blue cheese, avocado, and chives, with Cobb dressing. You can order it as an appetizer or as an entrée. Other appetizers are sweet corn bisque, beef carpaccio, blue lump crab crispy wontons, and ahi tuna. The entrée menu is rather extensive, so anyone should be able to find something they like: filet, shrimp and grits, vegetarian pho, chicken breast, salmon, Wagyu beef burger, and pork belly pastrami BLT. You can enhance your meal with a cold-water lobster tail, a grilled shrimp skewer, or pan-seared Georges Bank sea scallops. Disney Check meals are grilled chicken breast, whole-grain penne pasta, and grilled black grouper. Children can also opt for a hot dog, fish sticks, or grilled cheese off the kids' menu. Save room for a dessert trio—choose from mini grapefruit cake, banana-toffee cake, lemon cheesecake, warm blueberry cobbler, cappuccino brûlée, or dark chocolate crémeux with apricot marmalade and a white chocolate amber ring. Adults can order from the Derby's featured wine menu.

The Hollywood Brown Derby Lounge

DDP: No / Cost: $
TYPE: American; Lounge; Snacks and Drinks

Just outside the Brown Derby proper, you will find a small patio with a few tables. This is the Hollywood Brown Derby Lounge, a small, less formal version of the Brown Derby. You don't need a reservation to grab a table and enjoy shared small plates with your friends and family. If you have your heart set on the Cobb Salad, you can order it here, too. I also enjoy the artisanal cheese and charcuterie board, and you can also order all of the dessert trio options. This is a lounge, after all, so you'll see lots of specialty cocktails, beers, ciders, and wines. If you can't make up your mind, try a martini flight or a margarita flight.

I prefer the lounge to the restaurant. It feels too fancy inside the latter. The lounge is more upscale than most other lounges at WDW, but it's just a really nice place in the park to sit, people watch, and maybe even catch a parade or a nighttime projection show on the Chinese theatre.

Echo Lake

Echo Lake is modeled after the Echo Park Lake area of Los Angeles. In DHS, it's also home to a dinosaur slash ice cream shop, and a boat that sells hot dogs. For the record, the dinosaur's name is Gertie. This area of the park highlights

"California Crazy" architecture. Think life-size dinosaurs and a storefront shaped like a boat.

Echo Lake Kiosks, Wagons, and Carts

You can find all the usual suspects around Echo Lake: Mickey Bars, ice cream sandwiches, and frozen lemonade. Does ordering ice cream from the side of a dinosaur count as a kiosk, wagon, or cart? Well, no matter, you can get it from the side of Dino Gertie—who just happens to live in Echo Lake. Don't get your heart set on her, as she's only open seasonally. Stop by Peevy's Polar Pipeline to cool off with, yep, more ice cream. Peevy's also has frozen concoctions on their menu, like Coca-Cola Classic, Fanta Blue Raspberry, Wild Cherry, and Minute Maid Lemonade slushies. Adults can get any of those concoctions with a shot of Bacardi Rum or Tito's Vodka.

Backlot Express

DDP: One credit (Q) / Cost: $
Type: American; Quick Service; Lunch and Dinner

May the force be with your nuggets, burgers, and fries. This location is themed like an old backlot set complete with old props. Don't let the theming fool you—it's just your typical nuggets, burgers, and fries joint, only this time they slapped some Star Wars theming on it. Adding the word "galactic" or "Padawan" doesn't trick me, Disney.

If you wanted the full combo of nuggets and Star Wars, don't miss the Dark Side Chicken and Waffles: Darth Vader waffles topped with chicken breast nuggets served with maple syrup. You might need a Galactic Lemonade crafted with Tito's Handmade Vodka, guava and Odwalla lemonade if you decide to eat here. Finish your meal with one of the Star Wars cupcakes: Kylo Ren (topped with chocolate peanut butter buttercream icing) or BB-9E (topped with vanilla buttercream icing). Heed my advice—you should eat in a galaxy far, far, away from Backlot Express.

Dockside Diner

DDP: One credit (Q) / Cost: $
Type: American; Quick Service; Breakfast, Lunch, and Dinner

Dockside Diner was formerly known as Min and Bill's Dockside Diner. Apparently, Min and Bill got the boot this year. You mean to tell me that tourists weren't familiar with a 1930 American Pre-Code comedy-drama film starring Marie Dressler and Wallace Beery? Weird choice, Disney.

Breakfast is the most important meal of the day, and what better way to start your day than with a breakfast burrito, bagel, or cinnamon roll. Lucky for you, you can get all of these at the Dockside Diner. For lunch and dinner, grab a specialty hot dog of either the chili cheese or pulled pork variety. They also have a pulled pork sandwich and chili cheese nachos. Kids can get Uncrustables or Mac and Cheese. You can also order draft beers—Bud Light or Yuengling—or bottled Schöffergoffer Grapefruit Hefeweizen here. See, I told you it's not just found in Germany anymore.

50's Prime Time Café

DDP: One credit (T) / Cost: $$ (TiW)
Type: American; Unique/Themed; Lunch and Dinner

Don't you dare chew with your mouth open or put your elbows on the table here! 50's Prime Time transports you back in time to the era of June Cleaver moms and sock-hop Saturdays. The restaurant is located nearest dinosaur Gertie, and it's *always* busy inside. Don't let the crowd scare you away, though. It's well worth the experience. The waitstaff takes on the role of the nagging parent you never wanted, reminding you to mind your Ps and Qs, and that you simply have to finish your vegetables in order to get dessert.

On the menu, you'll find classic 1950s American comfort food: onion rings, meatloaf, fried chicken, and pot roast. Kids have the option of chicken tenders, mac and cheese, and pot pie. The Disney Check meals are salmon, grilled chicken, and meatless meatballs. Make sure you do eat all your vegetables, so you can order dessert. Brownies, apple crisp, and chocolate peanut-butter cake are some of the highlights. The most famous dessert here is the peanut-butter-and jelly milkshake.

"Dad's Liquor Cabinet" options are available to guests over 21—and if you don't get a reservation, you can always stop into the Tune-In Lounge, the bar attached to the restaurant. Fair warning—the lobby area and bar are typically crowded with guests waiting for tables, so even the seats at the bar fill up.

I love the theming of this restaurant, with the Necco wafer color palette, and the black-and-white TVs on each of the tables showing old family sitcoms. However, the first time my husband and I dined here, our waitress was totally not into her role. It was unfortunate seeing other tables getting the full experience and then ours was just meh. Mileage may vary.

Hollywood and Vine

DDP: One credit (T) / Cost: $$ (breakfast), $$$ (lunch, dinner) (TiW)
Type: American; Character Buffet; Breakfast, Lunch, and Dinner

My best friend has a 6-year-old niece who thinks she has her own YouTube channel where she reviews Disney restaurants. She does not. Her responsible mother thinks she's a tad too young for YouTube, but wants her to have an outlet. So, she points the camera at her daughter who then gives raw, unfiltered opinions to an iPhone camera. I've seen some of these videos. Her opinion is *always* eat at Hollywood and Vine. Now, this might be the consensus within the community of six-year-olds, but not so much for adults.

Hollywood and Vine is an all-you-care-to-enjoy buffet featuring the characters of Disney Junior: Sofia the First, Doc McStuffins, Goofy, and Jake from *Jake and the Never Land Pirates*. Sometimes, you might even catch Minnie Mouse making an appearance.

For breakfast, kids have their own buffet full of Mickey waffles, pancakes, and potato tots. Adults can get breakfast meats and potatoes, pastries, omelets, pancakes and waffles, and seasonal fruit.

Lunch and dinner have the same menus. For lunch, you'll see an array of salads, pasta, bread, fish, chicken, soup, roasted meats, peel-n-eat shrimp, vegetable creation (huh again?), baked treats, and soft serve.

The food isn't great here. But let's face it, the crowd going to Hollywood and Vine isn't going for the high-end food quality;

they're going to make their kids happy. If your kids are obsessed with Disney Junior characters, this is one of the only places to meet-and-greet them all at once. But, if they don't really care which characters they meet slash greet, you can get better quality food at another character meal (see: Chef Mickey's).

Commissary Lane

The smallest of the DHS lands. It's hard for me to even consider this a land since it consists of a walkway with two places to eat and a Mickey Mouse meet-and-greet. No matter, let's go!

ABC Commissary

DDP: One credit (Q) / Cost: $
Type: American; Quick Service; Lunch and Dinner

This eatery is a tiny step up from nuggets, burgers, and fries. It's meant to look like a real studio commissary, with a few TV show props peppered around. So, if you're a huge fan of *Grey's Anatomy* (a case with non-descript scrubs and a stethoscope) or *The Goldbergs* (watch out, a signed script from the cast!), you're in luck? The food here isn't much better than the effort they put into their prop displays.

The lunch and dinner menus vary slightly. Items such as burgers, shrimp, and ribs grace both menus. Kids can order an Uncrustable (Disney Check!), BBQ quesadilla, or mac and cheese (not Disney Check!). There are a few unique specialty cocktails, like a watermelon margarita and a drink called Happy Daze. Get it?! (I only drink Fonzie-themed drinks.) You can also get specialty cupcakes, in both Star Wars and Toy Story-themed varieties.

Sci-Fi Dine-In Theatre Restaurant

DDP: One credit (T) / Cost: $$ (TiW)
Type: American; Unique/Themed; Lunch and Dinner

The best restaurant in Hollywood Studios. Some may say that Brown Derby has better food and a classier atmosphere, and for that I won't argue. But for me, the reason I go to Disney World is to get the theming and design I just can't get at home. I can go to a nice restaurant at home. I can't eat boneless buffalo wings in a faux classic car watching the trailer to the Sci-Fi movie *The*

Horror at Party Beach at home. Now that the Great Movie Ride is gone, there are few spots left in Hollywood Studios that give you the taste of kitsch classic Hollywood—but Sci Fi still delivers. It is perpetually nighttime in the dining room, where you sit in a car like you're at a 50s drive-in, somewhere in the heart of the Hollywood Hills. Since the seating arrangements favor parties of two because you're sitting in a car, this is a restaurant where it's worth asking if they have walk-up availability for a party of two. You might just be happily surprised.

The menu is simple: many types of burgers, fries, shrimp, and sandwiches. My favorite is the appetizer trio with buffalo chicken bites, crab and shrimp fondue, and fried pickles. My husband and I usually split this as our meal. Kids can choose from mac and cheese, chicken tenders, and a cheeseburger. If you're looking for the Disney Check, look no further than beef skewers, shrimp and cheese quesadillas, and whole wheat penne. It wouldn't be a traditional 50s experience without a milkshake, and the ones at Sci-Fi Dine-In are truly out of this world.

Grand Avenue

The future entrance of Star Wars Galaxy's Edge lies in the periphery of Grand Avenue. Once known as Muppet Courtyard, this area, like much of DHS, seems to be in limbo. There isn't a cohesive theme that threads Grand Avenue together, but there are definitely places worth checking out.

Baseline Tap House

DDP: No / Cost: $
Type: American; Lounge; Snacks and Drinks

This is one of those places worth checking out. Baseline is one of the newer additions to Hollywood Studios and a great one at that. It has woven its way into my typical DHS day: O.K., let's ride Toy Story Mania, Star Tours, then Baseline? I would get a FastPass+ for this if I could! The beers all hail from the Golden State, and the bar itself is themed like you'd find it in the heart of industrial downtown Los Angeles. Choose a 16-oz or 22-oz pour, and if you want to try a few, create your own flight. Since this is a true tap house, everything, including the ciders, wines, and specialty cocktails, are on tap. If you aren't a beer drinker, but want to try the best of Baseline, get the California Sunset—a drink with Absolut Berri Açaí Vodka, Southern Comfort, orange juice, and sweet-and-sour with a float of pomegranate juice. You can also get some snacks and small plates. When this place opened, I was dying to try the soft pretzel. Sadly, it looks a lot better in photos because it tastes like it has been sitting under a heat lamp for hours. I was, however, delightfully surprised by the coffee-rubbed rib-eye steak puff with olive salad. It was like a classy, portable Philly cheesesteak. Baseline is a great place to hang out and drink beer. ♪ I wish they all could be California beers. ♪

PizzeRizzo
DDP: One credit (Q) / Cost: $
Type: Italian/American; Quick Service; Lunch and Dinner

Disney pan pizzas with a Muppet flair. Yes, this is your typical Disney quick-service pizza. It's nothing special. It's pizza pumped out for the masses. But, you may want to check this location out if you are a Muppets fan, because the theme is cute. Rizzo the Rat is your host extraordinaire. See if you can catch all the nods to the Muppets housed within Pizzerizzo. It's themed to look like your neighborhood pizza joint...if that pizza joint sometimes hosted weddings upstairs. You'll hear wedding reception favorites like Michael Jackson and ABBA piped overhead while you enjoy pizza, antipasto salad, or a meatball sub. Disney Check meals are a mini chicken sub and kids can also order personal pizzas and mac and cheese. You can also mobile order at this location.

Mama Melrose's
DDP: One credit (T) / Cost: $$ (TiW)
Type: Italian/American; Casual; Lunch and Dinner

Mama Melrose's is tucked in the very back of Hollywood Studios past PizzeRizzo. Legend has it, a young Sicilian starlet came from Italy to Hollywood searching for stardom. She cooked her family's recipes for her starving artist friends and quickly made a name for herself as Mama Melrose. She set up shop in an old studio space once used to house film equipment. Now you know.

Mama Melrose's serves fresh, Italian food with a California twist. You can begin your meal with a variety of flatbreads, minestrone soup, calamari, or Caesar salad. For your main course, choose from chicken parmigiana, spaghetti and meatballs, sustainable fish, wood-grilled chicken, and penne pasta. Tiramisu, cannolis, and gelato round out the dessert menu. If you can't choose one, try the sampler. Kids' Disney Check meals are grilled chicken breast, the fish of the day, and whole-wheat spaghetti. Other kids' meals are chicken parm, pizza, and spaghetti or penne pasta. Be sure to look at the Spaghetti and Meatball Cupcake on the kids' dessert menu—a chocolate cupcake with "spaghetti" frosting and a chocolate "meatball" with a strawberry "marinara sauce" and white chocolate "cheese." There's draft beer, wine, and if you're feeling particularly Italian, skip dessert and go right for the limoncello pour.

Mama Melrose's is not the worst place to eat a meal in Disney World, but it's certainly not the cream of the crop. If you are looking for good Italian food on property, Via Napoli in Epcot is typically my choice. But, Mama Melrose's is serviceable and does participate in the Fantasmic Dinner Package, where you pay for your dinner and get seating for the nighttime spectacular. Another good thing about Mama Melrose's is that, since it's tucked away in the back of the park, a lot of people forget about it, making it easier to grab a reservation.

Toy Story Land

Toy Story Land is the newest edition to Hollywood Studios. Shrink down to toy size and play with Woody, Buzz, and all their pals from the popular Pixar franchise. The land itself is rather small, with the highlight being the Slinky Dog Coaster. You'll also only find one place to eat here.

Woody's Lunch Box

DDP: One credit (Q) / Cost: $
Type: American; Quick Service; Breakfast, Lunch, and Dinner
Woody's Lunch Box has you covered if you are waking up early and fast-walking at rope drop to get on Slinky Dog Dash. Breakfast options range from the sweet to the savory. Have a breakfast sweet tooth? Get the s'mores French toast

sandwich—marshmallow and chocolate ganache stuffed in grilled custard soaked brioche encrusted with graham cracker crumbs. Lunch Box Tarts are a highlight at Woody's. Choose between chocolate-hazelnut or raspberry (think of these as a more refined version of a Pop Tart). For a more savory option, go for the breakfast bowl, a hearty portion of potato barrels smothered in smoked brisket country gravy, scrambled eggs, and a sprinkling of green onions.

Going to Woody's for lunch or dinner? The name of the game is sandwiches: BBQ brisket melt, grilled three-cheese sandwich, and a smoked turkey sandwich. The kids' menu also has a version of the grilled cheese and turkey sandwiches. If you aren't in the mood for a sandwich, get the totchos—potato barrels coated with beef and bean chili, shredded cheese, and signature queso, with tomatoes and corn chips finished with sour cream and a sprinkle of green onions. If you're just looking for a drink, there are a few specialty varieties of Joffrey's coffee here. Adults can get draft beer and cider or go for the grown-up's lemonade: Three Olives Cherry Vodka, lemonade, and black cherry purée.

Animation Courtyard

Make a right off Hollywood Boulevard and pass under the arch with director Mickey and his clapboard, and you'll find yourself in Animation Courtyard, home to the Star Wars Launch Bay, Disney Junior Live on Stage, Voyage of the Little Mermaid, and Walt Disney Presents. Once upon a time, this was the part of the park where you could see real Disney animators working on the newest feature films. Sadly, this area now only has very loose ties with its animation roots. Even more sad is the lack of available food here.

Animation Courtyard Kiosks, Wagons and Carts

Animation Courtyard is one of the most skippable areas food-wise in all of Walt Disney World. There's an ice cream cart and a popcorn cart. The only mildly unique thing about these carts is you may be able to find some Star Wars novelty products here.

Sunset Boulevard

Sunset Boulevard is located far below the looming shadow of the Hollywood Tower Hotel, and within earshot of the Rock 'n' Roller Coaster's guitar riffs. Mingle with the Citizens of Hollywood Streetmosphere troupe as you peruse shops and eateries reminiscent of 1940s Hollywood. The open-aired Sunset Ranch Market is the farmer's market of Sunset Boulevard, with each eatery selling a specialty food or drink item.

Sunset Boulevard Kiosks, Wagons, and Carts

The nature of Sunset Boulevard is grab-and-go. You won't find any sit-down restaurants in this part of the park, which makes the kiosks, wagons, and carts plentiful. You'll find a Joffrey's cart back by Tower of Terror as well as an ice cream cart. If it's ice cream you're looking for, skip the cart and go right to Hollywood Scoops. It serves tons of ice cream treats, from sundaes, to apple crisp, to the classic ice cream cone. The over-21 crowd can order a hard root-beer float. If you walk this way and find yourself in the Rock 'n' Roller Coaster Courtyard, you might see the KRNR Rock Station food truck. This truck sells hot dogs, chips, nachos, and ice cream. Talk about a sweet emotion.

Anaheim Produce

DDP: No / Cost: $
Type: American; Quick Service; Snacks

Re-energize with some veggies or fruit at this stand, which is part of the larger Sunset Ranch Market. This grab-and-go spot also sells pretzels, pickles, and churros. Anaheim Produce is my go-to for a walkabout beer. They sell Kona Longboard Island Lager, Schöfferhoffer Pink Grapefruit Hefeweizen, Angry Orchard Apple Hard Cider, and Magic Hat #9 Not Quite Pale Ale. Since they are also equipped with frozen drink machines, you can get margaritas, coladas, and seasonal frozen drinks, too.

Sunshine Day Café

DDP: No / Cost: $
Type: American; Quick Service; Snack

This eatery is only open seasonally. Gingerbread men and holiday cookies are on the menu, as well as an assortment of cold-weather drinks like Baileys Salted Caramel Hot Cocoa and the Peppermint White Russian. These are perfect for enjoying the Sunset Seasons Greetings, the projection show on the Tower of Terror that runs through the holiday season.

Catalina Eddie's

DDP: One credit (Q) / Cost: $
Type: American; Quick Service; Snacks, Lunch and Dinner

Catalina Eddie's specializes in single-serve pizzas. You can get your personal pizza topped with sausage and pepperoni, pepperoni, or just cheese. You can also add a side Caesar salad. The seating area is shared with other Sunset Ranch Market locations, and all of it is outside. If you are looking for generic Disney personal pizzas, go to PizzeRizzo. At least you'll be in air conditioning.

Fairfax Fare

DDP: One credit (Q) / Cost: $
Type: American/Mexican; Quick Service; Lunch and Dinner

Fairfax Fare is mostly Mexican food with a few American staples. Order empanadas or a fajita platter. You can also go for the Fairfax Salad with pulled pork, lettuce, bacon, fire-roasted corn-medley, tortilla strips, and cheddar, served with a jalapeño ranch dressing. Hot dogs can also be found on this menu—get yours plain or with chili-cheese topping. Disney Check meals include Uncrustables and a turkey sandwich. A few beers and mixed drinks can be found here as well as seasonal cupcakes.

Rosie's All-American Café

DDP: One credit (Q) / Cost: $
Type: American; Quick Service; Lunch and Dinner

Nuggets, burgers, and fries...and fried green tomatoes? Yep, this is a nugget, burger, fry place, but the dark horse on the menu is the fried green tomato sandwich. It's the main reason why people visit Rosie's: fried green tomatoes with jalapeño ranch dressing, pepper jack cheese, and tomatoes, topped with arugula on ciabatta bread. After you finish devouring this delicious sandwich, you can get a specialty cupcake or some strawberry shortcake.

CHAPTER FIVE

Disney's Animal Kingdom

Disney's Animal Kingdom is the last of the four main theme parks. It opened in 1998, and the name of the game here is animal conservation. At Animal Kingdom, you'll find animals of the past, present, and even a few of the fictional realm. There are many food options, and I'm happy to say they are some of the most unique at Walt Disney World. Yeah, you'll find some nuggets, burgers, and fries, but they aren't as pervasive as they are in the other parks. Follow me, adventurers, we're about to have a wild time.

The Oasis

The Oasis is the glorified entrance of the park. Unlike the other parks, where you can see the icon just by walking through the turnstiles, Animal Kingdom makes you work for it. Wander through lush garden paths covered by trees and observe a variety of animals in their habitats. Often there will be cast members on hand to teach you a little bit about the animals you see in the Oasis. Anteaters, wallabies, spoonbills, oh my! As you exit the Oasis, you'll see the icon of Animal Kingdom, the Tree of Life.

Rainforest Café
DDP: One credit (T) / Cost: $$
TYPE: American; Unique/Themed; Breakfast, Lunch, and Dinner

The Rainforest Café is located to the left of the park entrance before you pass through the turnstiles. You do not need park admission to gain entrance to this restaurant, but I'm not sure why you'd travel all the way to Animal Kingdom just to eat here. The Rainforest Café also has a location in Disney Springs. Inside, you are surrounded by rainforest animals and foliage. The restaurant is dark and a little noisy (the tropical storm that occurs sporadically through the duration of your meal can scare youngsters).

Unlike the Disney Springs venue, the one at Animal Kingdom serves breakfast. Hearty omelettes, waffles, flat-iron steak with eggs, or breakfast sliders may be a welcome change from Mickey waffles and otherwise typical Disney breakfast options. (Rainforest Café is not a Disney restaurant; it's owned by Landry's.)

The lunch and dinner menus are extensive for adults and children alike. Adults can choose from typical bar food like nachos or opt for a more filling dinner like Korean spicy stir-fry chicken. Either way, this is one of the largest menus in Disney World, and you're sure to find something for the pickiest or most adventurous eater.

The most famous dessert here is the Sparkling Volcano. Meant to be shared by at least three people, the volcano is a giant rich chocolate brownie cake stacked up high, served warm with vanilla ice cream, creamy whipped topping, and crowned with caramel and chocolate sauces. And served with a sparkler.

Not only is the food menu extensive, so is the bar menu. They have a full bar with tons of beers on draft, wines, and frozen concoctions. You can order these drinks if you dine-in at the restaurant but also if you find yourself at the Safari Bar, which is perfect if you just had a long park day and you want to rest your feet and have an adult beverage. You still get the atmosphere of the restaurant without having to wait for a table.

I don't understand people who eat at chain restaurants on their vacations, but I really like the Rainforest Café. The food is good despite the extensive menu, and the intricate theming is in line with Disney's standards. These restaurants came into popularity after I was the target child demographic, but if I were a kid going to Disney World, I would have begged my parents to eat here.

Discovery Island

Discovery Island Kiosks, Wagons, and Carts

You'll find a wagon with popcorn, frozen lemonade, and adult beverages in Discovery island. Also, no land would be complete without an ice cream cart. Eight Spoon Café is a small kiosk on Discovery Island right before you hit Asia. At Eight Spoon, you can order variations of mac and cheese: get it plain, with shrimp and sweet chili sauce, or with pulled pork. Another kiosk in this area is the Smiling Crocodile, offering two types of BLTs: a pimento cheese BLT and a turkey BLT—both are made on ciabatta bread. Pair your BLT with a Safari Amber Ale. If you're in the mood for a pick-me-up but don't like Starbucks, stop by Isle of Java for your coffee fix. You can also grab pastries and muffins here.

Nomad Lounge

DDP: No / Cost: $$ (TiW)
TYPE: African/American; Lounge; Snacks and Drinks

The Nomad Lounge is my favorite place in Animal Kingdom to grab food and drinks. It has a laid-back, relaxing atmosphere, with covered outdoor seating on the patio that overlooks Pandora, and there is lots of comfortable seating on plush chairs inside, too. No reservations can be made, so you can always walk in and look for an empty table. When you see one, grab it!

The menu consists of small plates that are perfect for sharing. Some of my favorites are the Tiffins signature bread service, which comes with three different kinds of breads: tadka, smoked baba ghanoush, and blatjang for dipping. The truffle poutine is worth writing home about. It comes with truffle tremor cheese, fries, crispy onions, and black truffle salt. The menu changes often, so it's worth making repeat visits.

We can't talk about a Disney lounge without talking about drinks. The Nomad Lounge offers many unique drinks that you can't find anywhere else on property. In fact, the Kungaloosh Spiced Excursion Ale Draft (brewed by Concrete Beach Brewery) was made specifically for the menu at Tiffins and the adjoining Nomad Lounge. My all-time favorite drink of the Nomad Lounge, and perhaps Disney World as a whole, is

Jenn's Tattoo. Okay, get past the name. It's not a good name. It sounds like something that's found at the base of a 40-year-old divorcee's back, but trust me, it's good. Jenn's Tattoo is made with Ketel One Vodka, watermelon, hibiscus, and lime juice. It is garnished with a candied hibiscus flower, and get this, the flower tastes exactly like a fruit roll-up. It's delicious, and even though it's on the sweet side, it's not sickening. My love for this drink allowed me to realize another really important factoid about the Nomad Lounge—to-go drinks. You can order your drink at the bar and get it to go. Better yet, if you get a table, add one more drink as you get your check. Jenn's Tattoo—bet you can't have just one.

Terra Treats
DDP: One credit (S) / Cost: $
TYPE: Gluten free/allergy free; Quick Service; Snacks
A small hut, only slightly bigger than a kiosk, wagon, or cart, Terra Treats serves healthy snacks. Hummus and vegetables, fruit, rice cakes, and buffalo chicken wings are on the menu, along with beers and ciders.

Creature Comforts
DDP: One credit (Q) / Cost: $
TYPE: American; Quick Service; Snacks
We made it through one full entrance land before getting to this park's Starbucks location, just past Pizzafari, heading toward the entrance to Africa. Creature Comforts has the same old Starbucks specialty drinks: coffees and teas to drink, pastries, fruits, and muffins to eat. There are a few AK-exclusive cupcakes, including the Tree of Life, Cotton Top Tamarin, Firefly, River of Light, and Zebra.

Flame Tree Barbecue
DDP: One credit (Q) / Cost: $ (TiW)
TYPE: American; Quick Service; Lunch and Dinner
Flame Tree Barbecue is a highly esteemed eatery in Animal Kingdom. I had never been there until I went with friends who swear by it. Now it's my go-to quick service in this park. They specialize in ribs, chicken, and pulled pork. If you want

to order something healthier, they have a watermelon salad with watermelon (duh), mixed greens, feta, pickled red onion, and a white balsamic vinaigrette. Be prepared to wait in a line if you go during peak lunch or dinner hours, or skip the line by mobile ordering. Flame Tree fans are as loyal as they come. The meat is melt-in-your-mouth good, and the portions are hearty. The seating area is outside under covered pavilions. Fun fact—if you look at the art carved into the pavilions, you'll see they represent the food chain. If you eat under the pavilions, keep your eye out for characters wandering around. I once saw Baloo and King Louie greeting guests in one of the pavilions, with no line to meet them.

Pizzafari

DDP: One credit (Q) / Cost: $ (TiW)
TYPE: Italian; Quick Service; Lunch and Dinner

Disney personal pan pizzas, a few flatbreads, and Caesar salad are all on the Pizzafari menu. This is the same homogenized pizza you'll find all over property. Sometimes Animal Kingdom feels as hot as the real Africa, and this is a rather large dining space. Luckily, Pizzafari's dining area is indoors and air conditioned. I think that's what speaks to the people. Disney Check meals are Uncrustables and Mickey pasta with turkey-marinara sauce. Kids can also get mac and cheese. There are two beers on the menu and one specialty drink that you can get with or without vodka—the Mandarin Orange Lemonade.

Tiffins

DDP: Two credits (T) / Cost: $$$ (TiW)
TYPE: African/Asian/Latin; Fine/Signature; Lunch and Dinner

Take a walk on the wild side at Tiffins, one of the newest restaurants in Animal Kingdom, and the only signature dining experience in this park. Influenced by Latin, Asian, and African flavors, the menu is truly unique. While there are more traditional items like surf and turf, this menu caters to the more adventurous eater. For starters, you can order charred octopus with Romesco sauce, olive tapenade, chorizo, and squid ink aïoli, or spiced chickpea falafel with mint-pistachio pesto, cumin-scented garlic yogurt sauce, and pickled vegetables. Main courses include crispy sadza with crispy corn cake, chermoula-infused spring vegetables, chakalaka with corn emulsion, whole fried sustainable fish, and pomegranate-lacquered chicken with sweet potato polenta, brussels sprouts, and citrus-fennel salad. You can add enhancements to your meal, but if you are on the DDP you'll have to pay out of pocket for them. Disney Check meals are grilled chicken, shrimp rice bowl, and cottage pie with seasoned beef, English pea, and whipped potato. There is also pasta marinara on the traditional kids' menu.

A tempting array of desserts include passion fruit tapioca crème, whipped cheesecake, a sorbet sampler, South American chocolate ganache, and guava mousse. Kids can order a chocolate brownie, Neapolitan macaron, or fresh fruit for dessert.

You'll notice the same alcoholic beverages from the Nomad Lounge menu, because they share the same kitchen. This gives you another opportunity to enjoy the splendor of Jenn's Tattoo.

Take your time with a meal at Tiffins. There are three dining rooms that are meticulously decorated with photos and art, many of which are a nod to the Imagineers who designed Disney's Animal Kingdom.

DinoLand U.S.A.

DinoLand Kiosks, Wagons, and Carts

As you approach DinoLand from Flame Tree, look for Trilo-Bites on the right. This stand sells buffalo chicken chips and milkshakes. If you want to take your milkshake to the next level, get the Smokey Bones Chocolate Shake with bourbon and candied bacon. You can also order beer here. Dino Diner might look like a canned ham trailer, but you can order an Italian sausage hoagie with peppers and onions. You can also order churros and cupcakes as well as draft beer and a frozen lemonade with Bacardi Black Razz Rum. DinoLand U.S.A. is modeled after kitschy roadside America, and what would America be without popcorn and ice cream? You will find these carts peppered throughout DinoLand.

Dino-Bite

DDP: No / Cost: $
TYPE: American; Quick Service; Snacks

Your favorite Häagen-Dazs ice cream flavors are served here—in a cone, sundae, or float. They also have the same buffalo chicken chips that you can find at Trilo-Bites as well as the classic Mickey pretzel.

Restaurantosaurus

DDP: One credit (Q) / Cost: $ (TiW)
TYPE: American; Quick Service; Lunch and Dinner

Obligatory nuggets, burgers, and fries spot in Animal Kingdom. You'll also find breaded shrimp items on the menu. At least the seating area is air conditioned. Disney Check meals are a turkey wrap and Uncrustables. Kids can also order a cheeseburger and nuggets. In summer 2018, Restaurantosaurus freshened its appeal by opening a lounge attached to the restaurant, and it is set for a trial run based on its success. It looks like a weird bunker and is open from 5:00pm until park close. They serve mixed drinks and light snacks. In addition to the mixed drinks, you can get fun non-alcoholic drinks here like the Teal Rex, Raptor Refresher, and Paleontology Punch.

Asia

Asia Kiosks, Wagons, and Carts

Instead of using one Asian country as a model, Disney imagineers call this section of the park Anandapur, which means "place of many delights" in Sanskrit. Animal Kingdom's Asia-themed land is meant to represent the blend of a several Asian countries. The backstory is that Anandapur was established as a royal hunting reserve that grew into a village. You'll see many kiosks that look like local vendors as you wander the walkways of Anandapur. Right near the base of Expedition Everest, you'll see the bright blue Anandapur Ice Cream Truck. This is my go-to ice cream spot in Animal Kingdom. They offer soft-serve cones and ice cream floats in chocolate, vanilla, and twist varieties. Drinkwallah, sponsored by Coca-Cola, sits across from Yak and Yeti and sells frozen Coke products and candied almonds and pecans. You can also add Captain Morgan to your frozen sodas. Warung Outpost is right near UP! A Great Bird Adventure Show and sells Mickey pretzels, cake push pops, margaritas, and something that's equal parts scary and enticing—the Triple Yeti Blast. This specialty drink comes with stacked layers of Kali River mango, Maharaja lime and Bali Hai strawberry margarita.

Thirsty River Bar and Trek Snacks
DDP: One credit (Q) / Cost: $
TYPE: American; Quick Service; Lunch and Dinner

You'll know you're at the right place by the screams of the nearby Mt. Everest Explorers. I'm not one for roller-coasters, so I consider this recent addition to Animal Kingdom my base camp. It has the typical treats: frozen lemonade, popcorn, ice cream bars, pretzels, as well as some grab-and-go breakfast items. The main appeal of this spot is the unique cocktails and beers. For essentially being a to-go counter, the beer selection is impressive. I enjoy a cocktail called Himalayan Ghost: Snow Leopard Vodka, guava, and lemonade. There is also the Khumbu Icefall with Cruzan Guava Rum blended with coconut and raspberry pureé or the Singapore Sling with New Amsterdam Gin, Bols Cherry Brandy, sweet-and-sour, grenadine, and Sprite. This spot is great for people who don't want to get on Expedition Everest and also a good place to grab a drink before you see Animal Kingdom's nighttime show, Rivers of Light.

Yak and Yeti Restaurant
DDP: One credit (T) / Cost: $$
TYPE: Asian-Fusion; Unique/Themed; Lunch and Dinner

The perfect place for conditioned air, fine food, and drinks. At Yak and Yeti, you'll feel like you're being treated to a meal in someone's private home surrounded by their personal collection of Asian artifacts. The main clue that you're eating in a restaurant and not a private home is the wide array of choices you will face when you're deciding what to order. You can start with small plates to share, like egg rolls, pot stickers, fried green beans, and firecracker shrimp. There are also larger appetizers that are meant to be split like ahi tuna nachos, lettuce cups, a dim sum basket, and a dragon roll. The menu has many varieties of noodles, bowls, and meals prepared via wok. If you're looking for something filling, try the Korean BBQ ribs or the soy herb-glazed rib eye.

Kids can order mac and cheese, cheeseburgers, chicken tenders, mini corn dogs, or teriyaki chicken breast. There are refreshing desserts that won't weigh you down, like mango pie and sorbet. The menu has an impressive selection of non-alcoholic and alcoholic drinks. There is also beer, wine, and sake. You can also go into Yak and Yeti just to sit at the bar area (this is separate from Yak & Yeti Quality Beverages, below).

Yak & Yeti Quality Beverages
DDP: No / Cost: $
TYPE: Chinese; Lounge; Snacks, Lunch and Dinner

If you want to try the drinks from Yak and Yeti on the go, here's your chance. This is essentially a window featuring mostly alcoholic beverages with a few food items like an Asian chicken sandwich, salad, and a turkey leg. For smaller bites, you can try egg rolls. Some of the most popular Yak and Yeti drinks are found here. May I recommend the Yak Attack? It's not nearly as gruesome as it sounds: mango daiquiri, Don Q Cristal Rum, and wildberry flavors.

Yak & Yeti Local Food Cafés
DDP: One credit (Q) / Cost: $
TYPE: Pan-Asian; Quick Service; Snacks, Breakfast, Lunch, and Dinner

If you wanted to eat at Yak and Yeti, but 1) don't have the time or 2) couldn't get the reservation, come here. They serve breakfast, too: breakfast burritos, bacon/sausage and egg sandwiches, and breakfast tacos. Even though Local Food Cafés shares the name with Yak and Yeti, the menu is a much more Americanized version of what you can get in the sit-down restaurant. The menu sports Asian chicken wraps, Asian Kobe beef hamburgers, American Kobe beef hot dogs, and vegetable tikka masala, along with sides of fried rice and egg rolls. Kids can order cheeseburgers, chicken strips, and Uncrustables. They also offer your typical alcoholic beverages: Bud Light, Beso Del Sol Sangria, and Safari Amber.

Africa

Africa Kiosks, Wagons, and Carts

What Anandapur is to Asia in Animal Kingdom, Harambe is to Africa. Harambe is the name of the village you'll find yourself traversing while in the African section of Animal Kingdom. It's a land with a lot of character, lively music, dancing, and plenty to eat. Caravan Road is a seasonal kiosk that sells teriyaki beef sliders and edamame when the park is most busy. You'll probably smell Mahindi before you see it—an oasis for popcorn and glazed pecans and almonds near the bridge to Discovery Island. The Dawa Bar is a great place to hang out and enjoy the atmosphere of Harambe. It's located right outside Tusker House and has a few high-top seats around a small bar. You can order an assortment of mixed drinks and beer. My favorite of the signature drinks here is the Takiti Punch, with Snow Leopard Vodka and watermelon lemonade. If you plan your visit to Dawa Bar to coincide with a Burudika performance (the musical group that plays in the village square), you are travelling Harambe like a true local. There's a small cart outside of Harambe Market called the Harambe Fruit Market that sells fresh pieces of fruit and prepackaged fruit. Mr. Kamal's is a small stand in between Africa and Asia that sells seasoned fries, falafel, and hummus.

Zuri's Sweets Shop

I had no idea who Zuri was before researching this project, but I'm definitely more apt to support her business of treats now. She started her first business in Harambe many decades ago and has since helped other women start businesses there. In her shop, Miss Zuri sells everything from bulk candy to exotic jerky. You'll see some of the typical Disney candy and cookies, too. Not only does she sell treats, but you will spot other African-themed souvenirs like cookbooks and housewares.

Kusafiri Coffee Shop & Bakery

DDP: No / Cost: $
TYPE: America; Quick Service; Snacks, Breakfast

Kusafiri is a spot to hit if you want a quick breakfast on the go. They serve wraps, "colossal" cinnamon rolls meant to share, muffins, and cereal. No breakfast would be complete without coffee, espresso, or cappuccino—good thing you can order those here, too. In the afternoon, they serve paninis and sandwiches: roast beef and cheddar panini, ham and cheese panini, smoked turkey sandwich, and a tomato and mozzarella sandwich.

Tamu Tamu

DDP: One credit (S) / Cost: $
TYPE: African; Quick Service; Snacks

This is one of the few locations where you'll find a Dole Whip outside of Magic Kingdom. What makes this one even more unique is that you can add alcohol to it! Add either coconut rum or dark rum to spice up your typical Dole Whip. If Dole Whips aren't your speed, go for a Malva Cake Sundae with vanilla ice cream, a Mickey ice cream sundae, a double chocolate-chip ice cream sandwich, or grab a handful of chocolate-covered espresso beans.

Harambe Market

DDP: One credit (Q) / Cost: $
TYPE: African; Quick Service; Snacks

If you are vacationing with a group, one of the worst feelings is not being able to decide where to eat. If you're in Animal Kingdom, look no further than Harambe Market. This open-aired, communal market is host to several stands which all sell a different food specialty. The four counters are Kitamu Grill, Famous Sausages, Chef Mwanga's, and Wanjohi Refreshments, serving between them a wide variety of foods like shave ice, ribs, beef and lamb gyro, roasted vegetables, pork sausage, grilled chicken, a Disney Check grilled barbeque chicken skewer, lots of non-alcoholic specialty drinks, and a few alcoholic specialty drinks and beers.

Tusker House

DDP: One credit (T) / Cost: $$-$$$ (TiW)
TYPE: African; Character Unique/Themed; Breakfast, Lunch, Dinner

Back in Harambe Village, you'll find the only character dining in Animal Kingdom, Tusker House. Enjoy an all-you-can-eat buffet and meet Mickey, Donald, Daisy, and Goofy decked out in their safari gear. Tusker House has the reputation of being one of the most enjoyable, overlooked, and underrated character dining experiences on property. The characters will parade around the restaurant and ask the kids to join them. The characters will also stop by each table to sign autographs and take photos.

For breakfast, you'll recognize some Disney staples: breakfast breads, cinnamon rolls, croissants, scrambled eggs, bacon or sausage, breakfast potatoes, Mickey Waffles, an assortment of breakfast cereals, and seasonal fruits. However, there are a few more unique items on the breakfast menu, including beef bobotie, frittatas, chutneys, and jungle juice.

The lunch and dinner menus are the same: breads and pitas, tabouli and hummus, spit-roasted chicken, roasted pork, basmati rice and curry chicken, curries, fruit chutney, and whole salmon. You'll also find desserts on the buffet like strawberry cake, fruit salad, brownies, and banana bread pudding.

There are a few American items for children to choose from on the buffet, such as mashed potatoes, corn dog nuggets, deli meats and cheeses, and macaroni and cheese.

Pandora: The World of Avatar

Pandora is the newest addition to Disney's Animal Kingdom. Opening in May 2017, this land was derived from the blockbuster movie *Avatar*. Geographically, while in Pandora you're actually visiting the Mo'ara Valley (adjusts nerdy glasses). You won't be able to miss the floating mountains and the lush foliage that grows all around you. Fun fact—when the imagineers were planning Pandora, they picked a lot of unwanted plants and flowers that were weird hybrids that most people didn't want. You wouldn't know that by looking at it, because Pandora is gorgeous and the attention to detail is obvious.

You'll find two attractions here: Na'vi River Journey and Avatar Flight of Passage. Na'vi River Journey is a relaxing ride down a river where you encounter the creatures and flora of Pandora. You'll also encounter the Shaman of Songs, the most technically-advanced Disney animatronic. Avatar Flight of Passage is the best ride in Disney World. Ok, that's subjective, but it's definitely has the longest line in Disney World. Don your 3D glasses, ride on the back of a banshee, and swoop over scenic vistas in this incredibly exciting attraction. There are only two places to eat in Pandora, but luckily for us, the Imagineers put as much detail into these unique spots as they did in the rest of the land.

Pongu Pongu

DDP: One credit (S) / Cost: $
TYPE: Na'vi; Quick Service; Breakfast, Drinks and Snacks

The story of Pongu Pongu goes that an expat fell in love with Pandora and decided to stay and open a drink stand. Ya know, tale as old as time. In Na'vi, "Pongu Pongu" translates to "Party Party," and indeed, the name fits. If you've never had boba balls, buckle up, because they are the main attraction here. They are gelatinous little balls that garnish the top of a drink and are usually fruit-flavored. The Night Blossom is one of the most popular items from this stand. It's made of layers of apple and desert pear limeade topped with passion fruit boba balls. Even though the Night Blossom is listed as a non-alcoholic beverage on the menu, you can add alcohol to it if you so choose. However, it's not combined with the frozen mix, it's poured on top, so make sure you mix it well and grab lots of extra napkins. If you want something else with alcohol, get the Mo'ara Margarita: Sauza Conmemorativo Añejo Tequila with strawberry and blood orange flavors topped with strawberry boba balls. One of my other favorite adult beverages here is the Hawkes' Grog Ale, a draft beer with notes of apricot and peach. Did I mention it's green? If I'm going to wait in the long line for Flight of Passage, best believe I am going into that line with (at least) one Grog Ale in tow. They do sell a few food items here as well. For breakfast, there's French toast sticks, sausage and egg biscuit, and Pongu lumpia—a pineapple cream cheese eggroll. Yep, it's delightful. After 11am you can order a soft pretzel to go with your green beer. Sivako!

Satu'li Canteen

DDP: One credit (Q) / Cost: $
TYPE: Na'vi; Quick Service; Lunch and Dinner

Satu'li Canteen offers fresh, somewhat-healthy options. Here you can choose a marinated protein which is served in a bowl over slaw and topped with boba balls. Choose from grilled beef, shrimp and noodles, grilled chicken, sustainable fish, chili spiced crispy fried tofu, or a platter of four proteins (for a whopping $74.99!). You can also get cheeseburger steamed pods, which are essentially a fast-food burger wrapped in a bao bun. Delish! Disney Check meals mirror the adult options: beef bowl, fish bowl, chicken bowl, and fried tofu bowl. Kids can also order the cheeseburger pods, a hot dog wrapped in dough, or a cheese quesadilla. For dessert, there is a chocolate layer cake and a blueberry cream cheese mousse.

There is inside and outdoor seating at Satu'li Canteen. Also, this dining location was one of the first to implement mobile ordering, which means they have it down to a science.

CHAPTER SIX

Disney Springs

In 1975, four years after the Magic Kingdom opened, a shopping and dining district named Lake Buena Vista Shopping Village opened on Disney property. The body of water surrounding Disney Springs today bears the name Lake Buena Vista. This area has undergone a few name changes, from Walt Disney World Village, Disney Village Marketplace, and then Downtown Disney. Downtown Disney encompassed the essence of this area for over twenty years: shopping, eating, and entertainment (R.I.P Pleasure Island). In 2015, an overhaul and rebranding of Downtown Disney was underway, which meant another name change for the area. Enter—Disney Springs. Disney Springs does not require any Disney park admission or separate ticketing, so it's more easily accessible. The two huge parking structures (free parking, I might add) support that fact. It's no hassle at all to drive to Disney Springs. You just park your car, eat dinner, and return home.

Marketplace

The Ganachery Chocolate Shop

Prepare yourself for a truly decadent experience at the Ganachery. It's pretty much anything chocolate that you can imagine. Expert chocolatiers are on-hand to answer any questions you have and to tailor your experience to your taste buds. You can watch them make these treats in real time. Some of the treats even have Disney character flair—like the house made s'more with Mickey's head in powdered sugar or the Sleeping Beauty dark chocolate bar. There is also the Chocolate Chiller, which looks like a Yoo-Hoo mixed with Baileys Irish Cream.

Goofy's Candy Company

Part-store, part-eatery—you can make your own candy creations here. You can purchase candy apples and cake pops crafted to look like your favorite Disney characters, including Sorcerer Mickey, Goofy, and Olaf. There is a case of cupcakes, cookies, and krispie treats to buy and eat or take home as souvenirs. A different slate of goodies is available depending on the time of year. Halloween and Christmas influences are prevalent in Goofy's, and you will not find a shortage of pre-packaged Disney snacks like popcorn, cookies and pretzels.

Aristocrêpes

DDP: No / Cost: $
TYPE: American; Quick Service; Snacks

This kiosk is located on the walkway over Lake Buena Vista near Goofy's Candy Co. They sell crepes and bubble waffles, an Instagram-worthy, currently trending food item. Think of it as a big waffle cone but instead of the waffle cone being square checks, the waffle indentations are circular and pop out like bubbles. There are two bubble waffles on this menu: salted caramel and strawberry. Inside the salted caramel bubble waffle is chocolate ice cream, pretzel pieces, whipped cream, crispy pearls, and caramel sauce. The strawberry bubble waffle consists of vanilla ice cream, fresh strawberries, whipped cream, and strawberry pearls. You can also order a s'mores crêpe, banana chocolate hazelnut crêpe, and a strawberries and crème crêpe. The menu isn't limited to those with a sweet tooth—the beef crêpe and ham and cheese crêpe are both deliciously savory choices.

B.B. Wolf's Sausage Co.

DDP: No / Cost: $
TYPE: American; Quick Service; Snacks

The Big Bad Wolf is back and this time, he's selling artisan sausages (and hot dogs) near Paddlefish (the restaurant in the big boat). Choose from the Italian sausage, Carolina BBQ hot dog, or Greek dog. You can also order the 3 Little Pigs Trio— small tastes of the Italian, Latin, and Greek all-beef hot dogs with a side of homemade pickles. Rest in peace, Practical Pig.

The Daily Poutine

DDP: No / Cost: $

TYPE: American; Quick Service; Snacks

If you can't get a reservation for Le Cellier, this is the next best thing for your poutine fix. There are four varieties of poutine here: classic, Italian (mozzarella and bolognese), Latin (fried yucca, black beans, pulled pork, and queso fresco), and French (mushroom cream sauce and gruyere cheese). They also have Labatt Blue and a Fireball Sangria with Beso Del Sol Red Sangria and Fireball Cinnamon Whisky.

Dockside Margaritas

DDP: No / Cost: $

TYPE: American; Quick Service; Drinks

You'll find on-the-rocks and frozen margaritas at this waterfront location, featuring sweet (strawberry), sour (lime), and spicy (habanero) flavors. There is always a seasonal margarita, so be sure to ask your server what it is!

Ghirardelli Soda Fountain and Chocolate Shop

DDP: No / Cost: $

TYPE: American; Quick Service; Snacks

This is probably the most extensive dessert menu in all of Walt Disney World. There are tons of sundaes (a few featuring Intense Dark 72% Twilight Delight Chocolate), shakes, floats, malts, scoops, and cones. A few non-ice-cream treats like brownies, cookies, and dipped strawberries are also on the menu. Dessert is not the only impressive thing about the Ghirardelli Soda Fountain and Chocolate Shop. The drink menu is also a sight to be seen, with cocoas, cappuccinos, lattes, espresso, and coffee. These drinks come hot or cold, with flavors such as hazelnut, caramel, and pumpkin pie.

Joffrey's Handcrafted Smoothies

DDP: No / Cost: $

TYPE: American; Quick Service; Snacks

Even though you will find coffee here and at most of the other Joffrey's stands around Walt Disney World, this location is best known for its handcrafted smoothies. You have your choice of such smoothie concoctions as Purple Piñata (apple juice strawberries, raspberries, blueberries, and yogurt), Flamingo Frost (pineapple juice, strawberries, bananas, and yogurt), and Razzy Jazzy (cranberry juice, strawberries, raspberries, and yogurt).

Florida Snow Company
DDP: No / Cost: $
TYPE: American; Quick Service; Snacks

Choose from an assortment of tropical shaved ice flavors. You can get your shaved ice in a flower cup and add sweetened condensed milk or sour spray for an additional cost. You can also order fresh roasted nuts.

Starbucks
DDP: No / Cost: $
TYPE: American; Quick Service; Snacks

One of the two Starbucks at Disney Springs, with the usual coffee, frapps, and refreshers. You can order breakfast sandwiches, wraps, and pastries all day. It is the most important meal of the day, after all. The Starbucks location on the West Side of Disney Springs has an identical menu.

Wetzel's Pretzels
DDP: No / Cost: $
TYPE: American; Quick Service; Snacks

Take a break from the Disney pretzels shaped like Mickey's head and try a Wetzel's. You can go for an original pretzel twist with warm dough and salt, or a bite-sized "Bitz" as they are so cutely called. Bitz might be better if you plan on sharing your snack. Both Bitz and pretzels come in pizza, cinnamon, sour cream and onion, and almond crunch flavors. The menu also includes a hot dog wrapped in a pretzel. The Wetzel's location on the West Side of Disney Springs has an identical menu.

Earl of Sandwich
DDP: One credit (Q) / Cost: $
TYPE: American; Quick Service; Breakfast, Lunch, and Dinner

This is a gem of Disney Springs, as indicated by its long lines throughout the day. The descendants of the actual Earl of Sandwich, John Montagu, are behind this eatery. Earl sells breakfast, lunch, and dinner. For breakfast, take your pick of hot sandwiches: egg and cheddar (with bacon or ham), ham and swiss, breakfast BLT, breakfast bowl, or breakfast burrito. He might be the Earl of Sandwich, but he can do made-to-order omelets, too!

For lunch and dinner, you can choose from salads, wraps, soups, and of course—sandwiches. My all-time favorite is the chipotle chicken avocado with grilled chicken, bacon, cheddar, avocado, lettuce, and chipotle sauce. Another famous sandwich here is the holiday turkey. No matter how hot it is, if my husband and I go to Earl of Sandwich, he always gets this sandwich. It's made with turkey, cornbread stuffing, turkey gravy, cranberry sauce, and mayonnaise. I've never been disappointed in this menu, and once you find a go-to item, it's hard to stray from it. Lighter options are available, like the Skinny Earl Quinoa Chicken Salad with field greens, grilled chicken, feta, quinoa, red onions, fresh strawberries, Mandarin oranges, and lite balsamic vinaigrette or the Skinny Earl Turkey Wrap with turkey, cheddar, romaine, Roma tomato, and light mayo in a whole wheat wrap. The dedicated "Just 4 Kids" menu consists of pizza bread, grilled cheese, a turkey and swiss sandwich, and a house salad.

Wolfgang Puck Express

DDP: One credit (Q) / Cost: $
TYPE: American; Quick Service; Breakfast, Lunch, Dinner

Looking for a high-quality meal but stuck in Disney Springs without an ADR? Look no further than Wolfgang Puck Express, which offers gourmet food for a relatively low price. The food is fresh, and the dining atmosphere is crisp and clean.

For breakfast, order an omelet, sandwich, waffle, or Corn Flake French toast, or go for the classic breakfast if that's more your speed (scrambled eggs, bacon or sausage, potatoes, sourdough or whole-grain toast). Lunch and dinner share the same prices and menu. Begin with either a butternut squash or chicken noodle soup, or try a Greek or Caesar salad. The sandwich section of the menu includes a whole wheat hummus wrap, bacon-wrapped meatloaf, chicken aioli, chicken salad, and a rotisserie turkey club. There is a plethora of pizzas for meat lovers (meatball, barbeque chicken) and vegetarians (pesto and goat cheese, roasted mushroom) alike. Quick-service locations are typically associated with grab-and-go options and less entrées, but WP Express has oven-roasted salmon, half rotisserie chicken, ravioli, and chicken alfredo to satisfy any level of hunger. Kids can order spaghetti, pizza, chicken tenders, mac and cheese, and grilled chicken mash. Desserts include a brownie, crisped rice treat, fresh fruit cup, cookie, cheesecake, and frozen yogurt.

Rainforest Café

DDP: One credit (T) / Cost: $$
TYPE: American; Unique/Themed; Lunch and Dinner

This restaurant is located right on the water near Art of Disney. The fiery volcano explosion gives it away. Other than the fact that the Animal Kingdom location serves breakfast, the location here and the location in AK are identical. Refer to the "Animal Kingdom" chapter for the full description.

Lava Lounge at Rainforest Café

DDP: One credit (Q) / Cost: $
TYPE: American; Casual; Snacks, Drinks, Lunch, and Dinner

The Lava Lounge at Rainforest Café is a waterside lounge with views of Lake Buena Vista, the body of water surrounding Disney Springs. They have a large selection of beers, with some local brews like Orlando Brewing I-4 IPA, Funky Buddha Pineapple Beach, and Floridian Hefeweizen. Signature cocktails capture the essence of the Rainforest Café: Blue Nile, Cheetah Rita, Mongoose Mai Tai, Strawberry Mojito, Panama Punch. There are also two signature martinis, the Blood Ruby and the Chocolate Kiss.

T-Rex Café

DDP: One credit (T) / Cost: $$
TYPE: American; Unique/Themed; Lunch and Dinner

T-Rex is essentially Rainforest Café in prehistoric times. This makes sense because both of these restaurants are owned by the same parent company, Landry's. They both are also prone to oversized aquariums. Say what you will about the novelty of

these places, but I've never been served unsatisfactory food at
T-Rex. The dishes are Dino-Mite (Disney's pun, not mine) and
the atmosphere is fun and unique. You get that same perpet-
ual nighttime atmosphere, even during lunch, and you are
surrounded by dinosaur audio-animatronics. T-Rex skews to
the younger demographic—namely, kids who think dinosaurs
are really cool. You probably aren't going here for the food, but
again, you could do worse.

In my next life, I want to come back as the person who
comes up with the names of the menu items of T-Rex Café.
Some of my favorites are the Boneyard Buffet (fire-roasted
rotisserie chicken, slow-roasted St. Louis style pork spareribs,
seasoned fries, and coleslaw), Jurassic Salad (celery, carrots,
tomatoes, black olives), and Raptor Rice (just how you imagine it). I guess the takeaway here is that the menu is large. The
appetizers range from a Supersaurus sampler (queso dip, brus-
chetta, T-Rexadillas, and onion rings) for four, to flatbreads,
to nachos. There are soups, salads, burgers, sandwiches, steak,
pastas, seafood, sides, and enhancements. I'd be remiss if
I didn't mention the dessert section of the menu appropri-
ately titled "The End is Near!" Two words: Chocolate. Extinc-
tion. It's for four people. It's cake, ice cream, whipped topping,
fudge, caramel, Butterfinger crumbs. I mean, how does any
mere mortal resist? There's also a Cosmic Key Lime Pie, Meteor
Donut Bites, and chocolate pudding cake.

Kids can choose from over twelve entrée options, with a lot
of the standards we've seen on other kids' menus: mac and
cheese, pizza, Jurassic chicken tidbits (nuggets). There are also
some other items we haven't seen on other kids' menus, like
lava lasagna and dizzy chicken (1/4 rotisserie chicken). Many
of the children's menu items refer to characters' names, like
Rocksy's Pasta, Sly's Slider, and the Dexter Corn Dog. Are we
supposed to be familiar with the canon of characters from the
T-Rex Franchise? Move over Pluto, Dexter's comin' through.

Adults can enjoy a bevy of beers, wines, and cocktails, either
to accompany a sit-down dinner or right from the Octopus
Bar—don't be alarmed by those huge purple and blue tentacles
hanging overhead.

4 Rivers Cantina Barbacoa Food Truck

DDP: One credit (Q) / Cost: $
TYPE: Latin/Mexican; Quick Service; Lunch and Dinner

Located near Earl of Sandwich, this food truck specializes in bowls, tacos, and quesadillas. Pick your filling: brisket barbacoa, pork sofrito, black beans and rice, chicken tinga, or tri-tip steak. Then, choose how you want it: taco cone, traditional tacos, burrito bowl, nachos, quesadilla, or with black beans and cilantro rice. They also offer a kid-size cheese quesadilla. For dessert, there's churro balls and chocolate hazelnut spread nachos.

The Landing

Erin McKenna's Bakery NYC

DDP: No / Cost: $
TYPE: American; Quick Service; Snacks

This is the place to go for the vegan, kosher, or gluten-free traveler. A wide variety of cupcake flavors are available for purchase: banana, red velvet, pumpkin, brownie. Or, skip the cake all together and get a frosting shot (seriously!). There are cookies, donuts, and tea cakes to satiate the sweet tooth, and breads, bagels, and biscuits available for purchase.

Jock Lindsey's Hangar Bar

DDP: No / Cost: $ (TiW)
TYPE: American; Quick Service; Snacks

Snakes, why did it have to be snakes? This is a question you hopefully won't be asking yourself when you wander into Jock Lindsey's Hangar Bar. Jock is the friend and pilot of Indiana Jones. The bar isn't that big, so if you see a table inside, grab it. There are also some waterfront tables outside. The inside decor is full of 1920s aviation and adventure—as is the menu. The signature libations are exotic and unique. You'll find references to Indiana's adventures all over the cocktail menu, like the cool-headed monkey (African rum, tangerine liqueur, lime juice, watermelon, and pineapple juice), and Shorty's Singapore Sling (gin, cherry liqueur, lime juice, pineapple juice, and grenadine). There are also a few fun libations without alcohol, like the Poisonless Dart with soda water, mint, simple syrup, and fresh lime juice. There are also a plethora of small plates and appetizers on Jock's menu. The Old World Pizza of San Marco is a great value. For $12, you get a deep-dish pizza topped with tomato sauce, basil, provolone, and pepperoni. It comes out on a flatbread board and serves more than one person. You can also order tuna tacos, pretzels, queso fundido, popcorn chicken, and pork belly sliders. This lounge is sure to bring out your inner adventurer—and if you skip it, you'd choose...poorly.

Joffrey's Coffee & Tea Company
DDP: No / Cost: $
TYPE: American; Quick Service; Snacks

We've dropped Joffrey's name during our trip to every theme park, but *this* location is Joffrey's home base. This set-up is similar to a Starbucks. It's not just a cart like you'd find in a theme park. You go up to the counter and order your beverage. The menu includes hot chocolate, coffee, teas, lattes, cappuccinos, and a few beverages with Grey Goose Vodka, Bailey's, or Captain Morgan toppers. I need to emphasize how many tea options there are here. It's nearly overwhelming! The flavors range from traditional (Earl Grey) to exotic (African Celebration with rooibos, almond, vanilla, herbs, and mandarin orange). Some of the hot beverages come with Disney character art in the foam.

Vivoli il Gelato
DDP: No / Cost: $
TYPE: American; Quick Service; Snacks

If you can't make a quick trip to Florence, Italy, this may be the next best thing. Vivoli il Gelato's flagship store is located in Florence and has been around for over 85 years. Their second and only other location? Disney Springs. Vivoli il Gelato specializes in gelato and sorbet. The assortment of flavors rotates, and you can also order your gelato in sundae and shake form. The birthday cake shake made with milk, yellow cake, and sprinkles in a chocolate-dipped waffle cone with sprinkles and whipped cream is a surefire way to celebrate any birthday (or unbirthday). You can also order Italian-style coffee drinks, like the frozen espresso shot or the Americano.

Cookes of Dublin

DDP: One Credit (Q) / Cost: $
TYPE: American/Irish; Quick Service; Breakfast, Lunch, and Dinner

Cookes of Dublin is the quick-service spot located next to and associated with Raglan Road, the lively Irish pub of Disney Springs. You'll find a fair mix of American and Irish specialties. Classic fish and chips headline the menu, and just to be clear, *chips* are French fries here, even when they are served with an Americanized cheeseburger. Warm, savory pies like beef and lamb pie are served with carrots, leeks, onions, and potatoes—or try chicken and field mushroom pie with leeks and potatoes in a creamy sauce. I guarantee Hog in a Box is not something you'll see on any other Disney World menu—it's slow-roasted pork shoulder with baby potatoes, sage and sweet onion stuffing, caramelized onions, and apple sauce. Kids can also order fish and chips, cheeseburger and chips, and battered chicken tenders and chips. Cookies and ice cream make up the dessert menu.

The BOATHOUSE

DDP: Two Credits (T) / Cost: $$$
TYPE: American/Seafood; Fine/Signature; Lunch and Dinner

Pretend you're the president of your local yacht club and dine at the BOATHOUSE. (Why all caps? WHY? I feel like I'm screaming!) The BOATHOUSE is described as Florida Surf and Turf. This dining location is on the water where you'll be surrounded by classic boats from the early 1900s. Amphicars (amphibian cars) will zoom past on the waters of Lake Buena Vista. Just in case you don't spend enough money during your dinner at the BOATHOUSE, you can charter a water taxi or a steamboat complete with a champagne toast and chocolate-covered strawberries.

Inside, the menu has surf, turf, and a delicious combination of both. There's a raw bar serving oysters, shrimp, lobster cocktail, crab and caviar, and several salads to start. You can also order soups, firecracker shrimp, calamari, and mussels. There are fish features like Korean-style BBQ fish tacos, Maine salmon, and ahi tuna. If you're really going all-in on a night out, get the original lobster bake for two: 1¼ pound whole Maine lobster, shrimp, clams, mussels, oysters, andouille sausage, red potatoes, corn on the cob, and BOATHOUSE lobster broth. If you're feeling more casual, and willing to get your hands dirty, order a dock side bucket: your choice of clam strips, fish of the day, or shrimp. They also have sandwiches like cheeseburgers, pulled pork, lobster rolls, and filet mignon sliders—though if I were shelling out two dining credits on an $18 cheese-burger, I'd be reconsidering my life choices. If you want more turf, and less surf, there are steaks aplenty: NY Strip, filet mignon, and ribeye. You can add jumbo lump crab to your filet and have it Oscar-style, or add a whole Maine lobster to any of your steaks. Kids can order grilled salmon, popcorn shrimp, a grilled chicken breast sandwich, a cheeseburger, and maca-roni and cheese. Don't miss out on the key lime pie in a Mason jar for dessert. If key lime isn't your thing, there's s'mores baked Alaska, whiskey caramel cornbread cake, and Florida Sunshine Cake (this serves four—yellow cake, orange cream cheese icing, and toasted almonds). The BOATHOUSE serves wine and a few specialty cocktails. One that is really calling my name is the blueberry lemonade, with Stoli blueberry, Deep Eddy Lemon Vodka, lemonade, and fresh blueberries.

The BOATHOUSE is a great place to celebrate the fact that you are vacationing on the water, in Florida, in Disney World. This isn't somewhere I'd pick on a whim. The BOATHOUSE was made with special occasions in mind.

Chef Art Smith's Homecomin'

DDP: One credit (T) / Cost: $$ (TiW)
TYPE: Southern/American; Casual; Brunch, Lunch and Dinner

Across the way from Morimoto Asia, you will find Chef Art Smith's Homecomin'. A Florida native, Smith has his roots planted in Disney dating back to when he participated in the WDW College Program in 1981. Since then, he has made his mark on the national food scene including being Oprah's personal chef for 10 years. The motto for Homecomin' reads "Upscale Down South." They partner with local businesses for fresh ingredients and offer farm-to-table ideals while never forgetting the mouth-watering details of down-home South-ern cuisine. The restaurant specializes in comfort food, so it is no mistake that the interior matches this sentiment. Homey wooden tables seated below large wooden beams provide for a casual and comfortable dining experience. There is also an outdoor patio area with wicker seats and views of the water behind the restaurant.

Lunch and dinner offerings don't differ in content or price. The menu specializes in southern classics like fried chicken, shrimp, and grits. Before I go into detail about the menu items, it should be said that the portion sizes are BIG. The appetizers are entrée-size, and the entrées are, well, ginormous. If you don't have a huge appetite, you may want to think about getting some items to share. For starters, you can order the Thigh High Chicken Biscuits (homemade biscuit sandwiches with fried chicken thighs, bread-and-butter pickles, and honey), Church Lady Deviled Eggs, or Ham & Jam Biscuits (similar to the Thigh High Chicken but with two types of ham, pimento cheese, and blackberry fig jam). Sandwich offerings include the featured Fried Chicken Sandwich (fried chicken, buttermilk-brined for 24 hours and double-battered, topped with lettuce, tomato, pickles, and hot sauce), and the Big Fish Sandwich (prepared with a locally-caught fish-of-the-day with varying toppings depending on the style and type of fish).

You may be sensing a trend with the sheer amount of fried food on this menu. However, they also offer a variety of salad options including a Spinach & Kale Chopped Salad (greens and grilled chicken tossed in strawberry poppy seed vinaigrette topped with strawberries, blueberries, crumbled goat cheese, and candied pecans). Of course, you'll also find a Fried Chicken Salad (which includes Art's famous fried chicken with egg, cherry tomatoes, fresh herbs, and cheddar biscuit croutons). Main-plate offerings, of course, include a platter of Art's Famous Fried Chicken (fried chicken prepared the same way as described above on the Fried Chicken Sandwich, served with a cheddar drop biscuit and creamy mashed potatoes). You'll also find staples like Shrimp & Grits, Fried Catfish, and the Chopped Pork Barbecue Plate (pork dressed with sweet and sour barbecue sauce served with a side of mac and cheese, and a biscuit). Other notable sides include the Grilled Corn Succotash, Carrot Soufflé, and the Southern Slaw. Kids' plates include fish sticks, fried chicken tenders, a fried chicken sand-wich, and cheeseburgers.

In addition to domestic and import draft and bottled beer, they also have local drafts like the Cigar City Jai Alai (Tampa) and the Funky Buddha Floridian (Oakland Park). Besides their delectable fried food, Homecomin' is known for its amazing moonshine concoctions. They offer 16-ounce moonshine cocktails or a 22-ounce cocktail which comes with a refillable squeeze bottle with Homecomin' coozie. It's $22 for the squeeze bottle and $12 per refill. Some of their specialty shine options include the Blue Hooch (Blue Flame moon-shine, lemon-infused moonshine, blue curacao, house-made simple syrup, fresh lemon juice, and a splash of Sprite) and the Rumshine Punch (Strawberry RumShine, blackberry brandy, banana liqueur, pineapple juice, and house-made grenadine). My favorite drink, however, you won't find on the menu. Ask them to make you a Purple Lamborghini, and you will get a mixture of the Blue Hooch and Rumshine Punch into one amazingly strong, dangerously delicious cocktail. You might notice a pop-up bar in the outside deck area of Homecomin'—you can refill your squeeze bottles here and actually take them with you around Disney Springs. Nothing like walking into Sephora suckin' down some shine.

Beginning in June 2018, Homecomin' began serving their Rise & Shine Southern Brunch on Sundays from 10:00am to 2:00pm. Starters include cheddar cheese drop biscuits, deviled eggs, and Art's house-made doughnuts (mini iced doughnuts with choice of bacon, pecan, and caramel topping or sugar, seasonal fruit, and cane syrup). Features include items such as the Hallelujah Biscuit (open-faced biscuit topped with fried chicken, over-easy eggs, bacon, pimento cheese, and sawmill gravy), fried chicken and doughnuts, French toast, and Hush Puppy Benedict (house-made hush puppy cakes topped with poached eggs, ham, fried chicken, and pimento hollandaise). All brunch entrées come with a choice of at least one side item. Kid options for brunch include French toast and the Junior Farmer Plate (two eggs any-style with choice of side). What would brunch be without some cocktails? Homecomin' offers several signature drinks to pair with their delicious brunch dishes. They offer several variations on the traditional Bloody Mary including the Garden Mary (Charleston Veggie Mix, Stoli Cucumber Vodka muddled with fresh limes and cucumbers garnished with celery, peppered cucumber ribbon, heirloom tomato, and banana pepper) and the Southern Mary (crop tomato vodka, Whiskey Willy's Bloody Mary Mix with pecan-smoked bacon, fried green tomato, pimento cheese-stuffed olives, and seasoned salt rim). They also have a white peach sangria, mimosas, and some specialty moonshine drinks.

The food at Homecomin' is absolute perfection, and it's somewhere I try to go on every single trip I make to Walt Disney World. My refillable squeeze bottle is always tucked away in my carry-on when I fly to Disney World, hoping for the chance to make a stop. I have always had excellent service here, and pardon the cheese, it always does feel like you're coming home.

Morimoto Asia

DDP: One credit, lunch (T) Two credits, dinner (T) / Cost: $$-$$$ (TiW)
TYPE: Pan-Asian; Fine/Signature; Lunch and Dinner

Across the way from Homecomin' is one of my other favorite restaurants on property—Morimoto Asia. Masaharu Morimoto is a Japanese Iron Chef. He is known for his unique presentation of food, and his restaurant in Disney Springs is his first foray into "Pan-Asian" cuisine offering selections of Korean, Chinese, and Japanese dishes. The restaurant itself is stunning. It's open-concept with high ceilings and a balcony overlooking the first floor. Long chandeliers glisten above, which somehow isn't out of place next to the exhibition kitchen, where you can see the chefs making your food before your eyes. A keen eye will spot a sushi bar on the upper floor, too. That's not the only highlight of the second floor, for it is also home to the Forbidden Lounge, a late-night lounge (actually, one of the places that's open latest in Disney Springs) with small plates and drinks.

Before we get ahead of ourselves, let's talk about the lunch and dinner menus. The menu options for lunch and dinner are similar, though there are several items that are only available for dinner (which starts at 5:00pm). Some items that are available on both the lunch and dinner menu get a slight discount during lunch. You are encouraged to share most of the menu offerings as they are all served family-style. However, you can also just get one entrée to enjoy yourself. The food here is amazing. The first time I dined here, the meal took about two-and-a-half hours. We took our time and perused the entire menu at our own pace. You can truly feel the love for food inside this establishment.

Morimoto Asia's menu begins with sushi and sashimi offerings. If you are narrowing down your dinner to sushi, go for the Sushi and Sashimi Pagoda which serves 2–3 people. You can start your meal with soups, salads, edamame, shumai, and pork bao buns. For your main course, try the mouth-watering Mongolian filet mignon, orange chicken, or Morimoto Peking duck. Rice and noodles dishes like duck ramen, Singapore laksa noodle, or Morimoto chicken-fried rice are a nice addition to share with an entrée. It's not a coincidence that the large circular tables at Morimoto have lazy susans in the middle. Your meal is meant to be shared! Children can order mac and cheese, mini ramen, bao wow (a hot dog in a steamed bun), orange chicken, or lo mein. Churros may not be synonymous with Asian food, but let me tell you, the churros at Morimoto are possibly the best you'll find on property. They are made in house with Nutella and vanilla cream. Other desserts are mochi mochi, sorbetto trio, or Morimoto parfait for two with chocolate cream puff, vanilla gelato, hazelnut chocolate crunchies, and sesame mochi.

There are specialty alcoholic and non-alcoholic drinks on the menu and plenty of wines and beers. My favorite drink is the Sake Sangria, made with sake, light white wine, plum wine, asian pears, apple, plum, and tangerine juice. As I stated earlier, since their Forbidden Lounge is one of the spots open the latest in Disney Springs, I recommend you save the best for last and end your night out at Morimoto Asia.

Morimoto Asia Street Food
DDP: One Credits (Q) / Cost: $
TYPE: Pan-Asian; Quick Service; Lunch and Dinner

If you want the taste of Morimoto without the full dining experience, stop by Morimoto Asia Street Food to get a sample of what the full menu has to offer. It's located on the ground-floor porch outside of Morimoto Asia, and the ordering area is a small window. There are a few outdoor tables that are considered dedicated seated for Street Food diners.

On the menu, you'll see spicy kimchi ramen, ginger chicken ramen, pork egg rolls, takoyaki (octopus fritter), California rolls, shrimp tempura rolls, and sesame lo-mein noodles. You can also try the famous Morimoto baby ribs: pork ribs, cilantro, and hoisin sweet chili glaze. These are the same that you would order from the menu inside.

I don't feel the same love for Morimoto Asia Street Food that I do for the full Morimoto Asia experience inside. It's not the quality of the food alone that makes Morimoto Asia an amazing place to eat; it's the atmosphere and service, too. You lose quite a bit of that charm when you order this food from a take-out window.

Paddlefish

DDP: Two credits (T) / Cost: $$ (TiW)
TYPE: Seafood/American; Casual; Brunch, Lunch and Dinner

This location has been a restaurant since 1977, when it was dedicated by Lillian Disney (Walt's wife) and called the Empress Lilly. You can't miss it. It's a Mississippi sternwheeler permanently docked on the shores of Lake Buena Vista. It has been updated to reflect a more contemporary atmosphere, with a sleek design throughout the bar and restaurant areas. No matter where you sit, you are bound to have a great view of the water.

The specialty here is seafood: clams, snow crab, lobster, mussels, shrimp, and king crab are all on the menu. You'll find unique twists on some of these items, like lobster corn dogs served with a sweet chili aioli. These are a great start to any meal at Paddlefish. Traditionalists can order a 1¼ pound Maine lobster. At lunch, you'll see more casual options like sandwiches (Cajun chicken, caprese, catfish, crab cake) burgers, and rolls (lobster and clam). There's plenty for the landlubber, too: filet, salmon, vegetarian pasta, pork, and prime strip. Kids can order filet skewers, shrimp pasta, a burger, grilled chicken, the fish of the day, snow crab, or a hot dog.

If you're in the mood for a nightcap, Paddlefish has a lounge on the top floor with indoor and outdoor seating. There's a special menu with appetizers like beef skewers, tableside lobster guacamole, ahi poke, and the Tower (king crab, jumbo Gulf shrimp, oysters, lump crab ceviche, and ahi tuna poke). The drink menu has wines, beers, champagnes, and some specialty libations. If you're feeling nostalgic, order the Lilly Spritz, named after Lillian Disney herself—it's essentially a rosé cocktail with strawberries and seltzer.

Paddlefish hosts a brunch on Sunday from 11:30am to 4:00pm. You can order a Monte Cristo, steak and eggs, crab and asparagus benedict, corned beef hash, an omelet, or the King Meets the Captain (peanut butter and banana-stuffed French toast crusted with Cap'n Crunch cereal and fresh berry compote).

Paradiso 37, Taste of the Americas

DDP: One credit (T) / Cost: $$ (TiW)
TYPE: North, Central, and South American Street Food; Casual; Lunch and Dinner

Paradiso 37 is located next to the Edison with views of Lake Buena Vista. This restaurant is one of the few that survived the transition from Downtown Disney to Disney Springs. It's lively and bustling, usually with musicians entertaining customers both inside and outside. The bar is structurally impressive, with a huge tequila tower housing over 37 varieties of tequila. Paradiso 37 looks and feels like a trendy bar, but you can also satisfy your appetite for North, Central, and South American cuisine here.

You'll need to carbo-load if you want to indulge in the tequila selections, so start with chips and salsa or guacamole. The South American Crazy Corn is corn-on-the-cob topped with cheese, and is meant for two people to split. If you want some northern exposure, get the Canadian poutine with cheese sauce, roasted garlic gravy, braised beef, and cherry peppers. For your main course, you can choose from fish tacos, burritos, salmon, enchiladas, Argentinian angus skirt steak with chimichurri, or a New York strip. You'll find a selection of fresh salads topped with proteins and an assortment of burgers and sandwiches that all come with fries that you can upgrade to white truffle or wasabi fries. Kids can order chicken fingers, grilled chicken, and grilled fish. Desserts include churros, tres leches, milkshakes, root beer floats, and the Paradiso Chocolate Stack: chocolate cake layered with creamy chocolate mousse served with warm caramel sauce and topped with vanilla ice cream.

Paradiso 37 has a full bar, but they also have a beer made specifically for this location, the P37, and American amber pale ale. You can order it in a glass or by the pitcher.

I feel as if Paradiso 37 is too often forgotten by WDW visitors. A lot of shiny new neighbors moved in around it, but it's still a good place to relax and grab a drink. You probably won't have a hard time getting a reservation here. In fact, you might even be able to walk up without one.

Raglan Road Irish Pub and Restaurant

DDP: One credit (T) / Cost: $$ (TiW)
TYPE: Irish; Unique/Themed; Brunch, Lunch, and Dinner

Cookes of Dublin and Raglan Road not only share a kitchen but also a unified feeling of authentic Irish hospitality. You'll find different menus for lunch and dinner, but the prices are the same on menu items that are shared between them. Try the classics for either lunch or dinner like fish and chips, bangers and booze (Guinness and onion sausage on potatoes with caramelized onion and beef stew), or shepherd's pie, and be sure to ask your server about the savory pie of the day. On the dinner menu, the entrées are extended to include cod, cider salmon, burgers, steak, and beef stew (with Guinness, obviously). Kids can choose from grilled chicken, fried chicken, mac and cheese, a burger, fish, and shepherd's pie. There are a few desserts to choose from: apple and peach crumble, bread and butter pudding, and chocolate heaven. Fancy more than one? Try the chef's dessert flight and sample a bit of everything.

Even if you aren't Irish, your eyes will be smiling after a visit to Raglan Road. There is nightly entertainment on the main stage (from 4:30pm to 1:00am) as well as the patio stage (from 8:00pm to 12:30am). The Rhythms of Raglan Dance Show is a mix of musicians with accompanying dancers who perform in a 90-minute show on the main stage. Children are encouraged to join them for dancing. There is a late-night menu here as well. Speaking of late-night, does one really go to an

Irish pub if they don't order a beer? You'll of course find beers like Guinness and Smithwick's, but Raglan Road has a pretty massive selection of domestic beers, too.

Brunch is all the rage in Disney Springs nowadays, so Raglan Road had to get in on the action. On Saturdays and Sundays, get your brunch on at Raglan Road. You'll see many of the entrées from the lunch and dinner menus make their way to the brunch menu. If savory brunches are your thing, Raglan is the way to go. What would Sunday Funday be without some boozy brunch beverages? Try the Cure (house made Bloody Mary), the Grapefruit and T (Raglan's spin on a gin and tonic with crushed grapefruit), or the Strawberry Fields Mimosa (vodka, Aperol, lemon juice, strawberry puree, and prosecco). A mimosa with vodka? Sign me up.

Wine Bar George
DDP: One credit (T) / Cost: $$
TYPE: Spanish/American; Casual; Lunch and Dinner

Master sommelier George Miliotes is the namesake for this Spanish-estate-style eatery, one of the newest editions to Disney Springs, opening in the summer of 2018. While George is in charge of the wine, executive chef Ron Rupert is at the helm for food. Chef Rupert has roots in Disney World—he helped open Jiko at Animal Kingdom Lodge. The décor of this restaurant is industrial. You'll see exposed air vents and brick walls. Wine Bar George has two stories, the second being quieter than the first. On the first floor, you'll notice the central bar with the impressive array of bottles hanging above. In addition to the bar, there are several high-top tables where you can sit.

Wine Bar George serves lunch and dinner with only slight variations between the two. Surprisingly, you'll find more options at lunch with a dedicated "Lunch Plates" section. You can order a chicken salad sandwich, skirt steak with fries, and a BLT+C, which is a bacon, lettuce, tomato, brioche, four-cheese sauce, and homemade chips. Both the lunch and dinner menus feature small plate options with hummus, crispy mac and cheese bites, octopus salad, spiced olives, and porchetta-spiced pork cheeks, to name a few. Borrowing from the Spanish-style of eating tapas, there are several options for charcuterie boards.

Instead of a traditional entrée intended for one guest, Wine Bar George serves their entrées family-style, for 2–4 people. You can choose from the skirt steak with potatoes, chimichurri and vegetables, sea bass, or a wine-braised chicken. Kids can order meatballs, mac and cheese, and chicken tenders.

Your clever sleuthing skills may have led you to believe that the restaurant is named Wine Bar George because of the prevalence and importance of wine on this menu. You'd be right. Even though there are beers and mixed cocktails, the wine list is expansive. Not a seasoned wine drinker? The staff can lead you to a wine best-suited to your tastes. You can order some of the wines in one-ounce pours, while others come by the glass or by the bottle. There is also a selection of wines on tap. And don't miss the sangria. On his menu, George notes that "Spain is the single greatest country to find unique, delicious, and affordable wines." Wow, something in Disney bragging about affordability? George, to that I say, cheers!

The Basket at Wine Bar George
DDP: One credit (Q) / Cost: $
TYPE: Spanish/American; Quick Service; Snacks, Lunch, and Dinner
Stop by the Basket for all your gourmet picnic needs. Yeah, picnic needs. You won't find something like this anywhere else on WDW property. You can order your wines to go by the glass or by the carafe. You can order the Picnic Basket for 4 which includes olives and hummus, choice of two cheese and charcuterie boxes, choice of one sandwich, four chocolate chip cookies, and wine. It's available for two as well, if you don't need as much food. You can also order sandwiches or get one of their boxed light options like olives and hummus, calabrese, brie, honey, crackers, or sopressata, cheddar, fig, and crackers.

STK Orlando
DDP: One credit, lunch (T) Two credits, dinner (T) / Cost: $$-$$$$ (TiW)
TYPE: Steaks/Seafood; Fine/Signature; Brunch, Lunch, and Dinner
Not your daddy's steakhouse—yeah, I didn't make that up. That's STK's actual slogan. STK has a cool, metropolitan feel with prices to match the big city. I always take the "Disney premium" into account when I talk about dining in Disney, but

STK is elevated beyond that. It's a great place for a special celebration, but it comes at a price. STK specializes in—what else?
Can I buy some vowels? STEAK. This franchise has locations in
Atlanta, Denver, Chicago, Ibiza, Vegas, London, Los Angeles,
Milan, NYC, South Beach, Toronto, San Diego, Mexico, Dubai...
and now Disney Springs. It boasts an upscale steakhouse menu,
with a fun, lounge atmosphere. I will warn you that many report
that dinner at STK is too loud. There is often a DJ during dinner
hours. This isn't your daddy's steakhouse, after all. If you are
looking for a quieter experience, procure a lunch reservation.

Whether you go for lunch or dinner, you'll find the same
simple, steak specialties, such as a 6 or 10 oz. filet, a 14 oz. NY
strip, or a 16 oz. cowgirl ribeye. You can spice up your steak with
additions like peppercorn crust, truffle butter, shrimp, crab,
or lobster. At dinner, the offerings are somewhat expanded,
and include a dry-aged bone-in sirloin, a dry-aged Delmon-
ico, dry-aged porterhouse (meant to be shared between two
people), and finally, a dry-aged tomahawk ribeye—clocking in
at a whopping $128, at press time. If red meat isn't your thing,
there are a few options like pan-roasted chicken, roasted cauliflower "steak," seared tuna, salmon, and lobster with grits. The
lunch entrées are more dressed down: a Waygu beef hot dog,
spiced tuna bowl, burgers, and sandwiches. The raw bar at STK
has oysters, shrimp cocktail, ceviche, and king crab. Sides such
as truffle fries, mac and cheese (with or without lobster), creamy
Yukon potatoes, jalapeño cheddar grits, and sweet corn pudding
can be ordered à la carte and shared with your party. Kids can
order chicken fingers, chicken breast, crispy mahi fingers, mac
and cheese, or the Kid's STK—a filet with hand-cut fries.

STK also hosts brunch on Saturdays and Sundays. Begin
with an order of iced cinnamon monkey bread. The entrées
are crab cakes benedict, fried chicken and funnel cake, lemon
ricotta pancake, and old-school eggs, bacon, and potatoes.
No brunch would be complete without cocktails, so wet your
whistle with a mimosa, a Cucumber Stiletto (with Ketel One
citroen, St. Germain, muddled cucumber, and mint), or Frosé
(local raspberry sorbet dropped into a glass of chilled rosé).

Instead of happy hour, STK has social hour at their lounge:
3:30pm to 6:00pm on weekdays and 10:00pm to close on

Thursdays, Fridays, and Saturdays. It's half-off drinks, and "deals" (yes, I understand, relative term) on small plates such as tuna tartare tacos, smoked bacon skewers, tater tots, hummus, and jalapeño cheddar grit croquettes. The drink menu at the bar is extensive: beer, wine, champagne, and lots of specialty cocktails. The "...Not Your Daddy's Manhattan" is made of Bulleit bourbon, zinfandel port, Carpano Antica sweet vermouth, and bitters. If you're looking for something sweeter, go for the strawberry cobbler with Belvedere, fresh muddled strawberry, and graham cracker crust.

The Edison

DDP: One credit (T) / Cost: $$
TYPE: American; Casual; Lunch and Dinner

Designed to look like a 1920s electric company, the Edison has perfected the look of gothic, steampunk décor. This multi-story restaurant has 35-foot ceilings and several different eating sections, like the Tesla Lounge, the Ember Parlour, and the Radio Room. There is often live entertainment like aerialists and DJs.

The lunch and menu dinners vary slightly in content but not in price. On both, you'll see shared plates like deviled eggs, salads, burgers, grilled cheese, and a Coney Island Diner Dog. For dinner, a few heartier options are peppered in, like the old-fashioned meatloaf and gravy, BBQ sirloin steak tips, Scottish salmon, and 28 day dry-aged prime rib. Kids can choose a burger (with or without cheese), tomato soup and grilled cheese, or chicken tenders as their entrée here.

There are desserts to share like the Great Big Rocky Road Shake with chocolate gelato, white chocolate drizzle, cinnamon-chile spiced chocolate syrup, whipped cream, candied almonds, marshmallows, and chocolate chip, or the Lollipop Tree with cheesecake pops and bubble gum whipped cream. You can also go on a solo mission for your dessert with mousse cake, apple cobbler, ice cream, and sherbets.

While there is a beer and wine menu, there is also a carefully crafted cocktail menu. You'll find drinks here you won't find anywhere else on property, like the Samantha Sterling, made with Grey Goose vodka, Lillet Rose, lime, watermelon juice, and cinnamon cordial. Or, you can order the Edison, with bourbon, belle de brillet pear brandy, lemon, and honey cordial.

If you have your heart set on going to the Edison, skip this paragraph. I have been there once, and I wanted to go for the sole purpose of trying out the cocktail menu shortly after they opened. It was not a peak time of day, so there were no acrobats or contortionists, and the restaurant wasn't that busy. Our waiter was strange—not rude, not overly friendly, just strange. Most of the drinks on their signature cocktail menu have a bit of a kick to them, and I don't think I would consider any of them "girly" drinks. After the ladies in our party ordered, the waiter wanted to be sure the females present read the description because "they are really hard drinks." Well, if your drinks aren't made for over half of the population, I'll go to one of the other great places to eat and drink in Disney Springs. Also, the appetizers were underwhelming. Not horrible, just not great for the price paid. My party was prepared to order a few drinks here and linger—but after one, we decided to cash out. Will I go back? Probably. I don't want to write it off after only one experience. I'll give them a fair shake sometime and go back for dinner.

Maria and Enzo's Ristorante

DDP: One credit (T) / Cost: $$
TYPE: Italian; Casual; Brunch (Sunday only), Lunch, and Dinner

Even though you'll feel like you're in an airport terminal, the fare here is *much* better than typical airport food. Maria and Enzo's is an open, airy restaurant with tall ceilings and a vintage, 1930s Art Deco airport terminal décor. You'll have unobstructed views of Lake Buena Vista. The food here is Italian—specifically Sicilian. The restaurant serves lunch and dinner daily with the exception of Sundays when they swap out their lunch offerings for their specialty brunch.

This is one of those restaurants where you see a price reduction in lunch compared to dinner. You'll also spot slight differences in the lunch and dinner menu offerings. Choose from an antipasti trio with arancini, mozzarella caprese, and prosciutto di parma, or one of the several fresh salads like fennel and orange salad, and a chopped salad that is only on the lunch menu. Pasta options include classic spaghetti and meatballs, linguini and clams, and three-cheese ravioli. For dinner, you can try the Sicilian oven-baked pasta. Snapper and ahi tuna are both lunch and dinner entrées. The dinner menu has two steak options missing from the lunch menu: dry-aged rib-eye and a NY strip steak. The dinner menu also has a dedicated "Parmigiana" section with both chicken and eggplant. You'll find a typical slate of Italian desserts on the menu: cannoli, torta, gelato, sponge cake, and sorbet. There is no separate menu for children.

I mentioned that on Sundays, Maria and Enzo host a brunch. The brunch menu offers much of the same as the lunch and dinner menus, but there are a few entrées that are considered more breakfast-oriented. There is a prix-fixe menu where you choose one of the following entrées: French toast, farmstead vegetable frittata, spaghetti alla carbonara, New York strip steak and eggs, or poached hen egg and quinoa-kale salad. If you decided to do the prix-fixe menu, you also get access to the buffet which has salami and cheese, pizza, antipasti, yogurt, assorted pastries, and jumbo shrimp cocktail. The buffet part of brunch was so good, I wish there had been an option just to have it with no entrée. For dessert, the prix-fixers can dip graham crackers, fruit, and marshmallow into a chocolate fountain. You can also add endless mimosas or peach bellinis to your meal (it doesn't matter if you do the prix-fixe or order off the menu) for an additional cost. It should be noted that you have to commit to only mimosas or only peach bellinis. You can't mix and match if you get bottomless drinks.

Pizza Ponte

DDP: One credit (Q) / Cost: $$
TYPE: Italian; Quick Service; Lunch and Dinner

Pizza Ponte is Disney Springs' answer to authentic pizza offerings. The menu is simple—pizza by the slice in a few varieties: tomato, mushrooms, porchetta, 4-cheese, and spicy salame. There are also sandwiches like prosciutto and cheese, tomato and mozzarella, muffuletta, ham and cheese, and Sicilian tuna, and there are way more desserts than you would expect from such a simple menu: cannolis, pistachio and mascarpone parfait, biscotti, zeppola con panna, Italian-style cookies, and limoncello parfait.

Enzo's Hideaway

DDP: One credit (T) / Cost: $$
TYPE: Italian; Unique/Themed; Lunch and Dinner

It will be hard to hide my delight for Enzo's Hideaway, so be warned. This new addition to Disney Springs is meant to be a Prohibition-style tunnel bar hidden under the hustle and bustle of Disney Springs. It's easy to miss the entrance (hence the "hideaway"). The interior has brick walls and comfortable, red booths. There is a bar with high-top seating, and a large marble, communal-style table where one large party can sit or several small parties. The wine selection is impressive, and Enzo's has a sommelier on-hand for tastings and recommendations.

While the emphasis of this location is the lounge and wine cellar, do not overlook the food menu. This is some of the best food in Disney Springs and Walt Disney World in general. I am still dreaming (and coincidentally, drooling) over the last time I had the Dolce Vita, a platter of cured meats and cheeses: prosciutto, salami, finocchiona, parmigiano-reggiano, pecorino Romano, fontina d'Aosto, olives, pickled veggies, breadsticks, and mustard fruit. They also have two pre-set meals—a prix-fixe lunch with a choice of soup or Caesar salad and a choice of spaghetti bolognese, chicken parmesan, or mussels fra diavola as your main course. There's a Sunday Supper (available only on Sundays from 4:00pm to 10:00pm) consisting of an anti-pasto board and salad, meats, rigatoni, and assorted sweets and ice cream. Most notably, there's no corking fee for wine so you can bring your own. There are many items to order à la carte: rigatoni, linguini, classic lasagna, eggplant parmesan, sea bass, salmon, and grilled sirloin. The traditional Italian desserts available include gelati, tiramisu, cannolis, and a mocha sundae. Kids have the choice of spaghetti and meatballs, chicken parmesan, or four cheese pasta.

In addition to the traditional lunch and dinner menus, Enzo's has a late-night bites menu, featuring meats and cheeses, meatball sliders, and caprese. But, let's keep Enzo's our little secret, okay?

Town Center

Amorette's Patisserie

DDP: No / Cost: $

TYPE: American; Quick Service; Snacks

This pastry shop is sure to delight your eyes and your taste buds. All of the treats under the glass are beautiful to behold. They run the gamut from New York cheesecake, key lime tarts, éclairs, crème brûlée, and the Mickey Mousse, a small chocolate chiffon cake with dark chocolate mousse and white chocolate mousse that looks just like Mickey. Speaking of characters, be sure to take a look at the dome cakes modeled to look like Mickey, Minnie, Donald, Goofy, and Pluto. These treats are fully conceptualized, and you can even see art on the wall similar to storyboards for some of the pastries. There are a few savory items like turkey or ham on focaccia, crepes, and a vegetable croissant. My favorite thing to get at Amorette's Patisserie is the wine slushy. It comes in a strawberry shiraz flavor or a mango Moscato flavor. The strawberry shiraz is really sweet, and the mango is tart, but mixed together they are perfection.

Blaze Fast-Fire'd Pizza

DDP: No / Cost: $

TYPE: American; Quick Service; Snacks, Lunch, and Dinner

Located behind D-Luxe Burger or across the walking bridge near Homecomin', you will find Blaze. Open for lunch and dinner, this quick service restaurant offers their signature "fast-fire'd" 11" artisanal pizzas with over 40 toppings to choose from. Blaze Pizza features a contemporary style with both indoor and outdoor seating. Think of Blaze as similar to a Subway but with pizzas instead of sandwiches. As you may be able to tell by the name, these pizzas bake extremely quickly as they are cooked in a high-temperature, open-flame oven. Most personal pizzas cook in under 5 minutes. You can choose to build your own personal pizza by choosing between high-rise or gluten free dough, then choosing your sauces, cheese, and toppings. If that kind of on-the-spot decision making isn't your style, you can pick from some of their signature pizza creations including the Red Vine (Ovalini mozzarella, cherry tomatoes, parmesan, basil, red sauce, and olive oil drizzle) or the Link In (sausage, red peppers, sautéed onions, mozzarella, and red sauce). Also available are simple salads in both side or entrée portions with the option to add a choice of protein. For dessert, be sure to try the specialty S'more Pie. Drink options include blood orange lemonade as well as assorted draft and bottled beers, and wine.

Coca-Cola Store Rooftop Beverage Bar
DDP: No / Cost: $
TYPE: American/Global; Quick Service; Drinks

High atop the Coca-Cola Store near the Lime parking garage is Rooftop Beverage Bar, serving Coke products from around the world. You can take the elevator to get up to the bar, or you can trek inside the perimeter of the building and walk to the rooftop. Once you're there, take in the views of Disney Springs. This is a Coke fan's mecca: fountain beverages, freestyle machines, glass bottles, flavored water, coffee, tea, energy drinks, juices, floats, ICEEs, smoothies, flights, mocktails, and cocktails. I really like it because, like Walt Disney's vision for Disneyland, this is a place where parents and kids can have fun together. A popular choice here is the "Coca Cola Tastes of the World," a tray of 16 Dixie Cup-sized cups filled with either Coca-Colas from around the world, a combo with 8 international and 8 domestic, or a tray of all floats. This is a fun and unique experience for families or groups of friends. For adults, there's a range of cocktails to choose from, all of which have a Coca-Cola product mixed in. My favorite is the Cherry Coke Ripper: Malibu Rum, Evan Williams Cherry Whiskey, and Cherry Coke. There is also a Vanilla Russian on with Stoli vodka, Kahlua, and Vanilla Coke. You can, of course, order the tried-and-true Jack and Coke. There are also traditional or signature cocktail flights. There isn't much food on the menu. It's limited to snacks: brownies, pretzels, peanuts, cake, and popcorn.

D-Luxe Burger
DDP: No / Cost: $
TYPE: American; Quick Service; Snacks, Lunch, and Dinner

Located across from Blaze pizza, D-Luxe is a meat lovers' paradise, with a bevy of burgers to choose from. There are classic options like the Super Triple Burger with three 3 oz. burgers topped with cheddar cheese, bacon, lettuce, tomato, pickles, and onions. There is also the classic cheeseburger with all of the toppings listed above on one patty. For the more adventurous palette, choose one of the premium burgers like the Southern (topped with fried green tomato, pimento, lettuce, grilled onion, and bacon) or the El Diablo (chorizo- and beef-blend patty, fried banana peppers, pepper jack cheese, lettuce, tomato, grilled onion, and chipotle mayonnaise). Various "duos" include two burgers and fries and two fountain beverages. Kids can order burgers or nuggets, and there is a ground chicken burger as a Disney Check item. You'll find a boatload of gelato shakes with flavors like s'mores, salted caramel, strawberry shortcake, and pumpkin pie. There is also a totally separate menu space for alcoholic takes on the gelato shake, like the Smoked Bourbon and the Godiva Chocolate and Strawberry Malt. D-Luxe Burger also has a secret menu specifically for customers who use mobile ordering. This menu features a bacon-and-blue burger, BLT, and grilled cheese sandwich which aren't on the menu if you simply walk up and order.

The Polite Pig

DDP: No / Cost: $$
TYPE: American Barbecue; Quick Service; Lunch and Dinner

The Pig is owned by local chefs James, Julie, and Brian Petrakis, and is the only dining location in Disney Springs owned and operated by Orlando natives. They also own the Ravenous Pig, DoveCote Brasserie, and Cask and Larder. The menu holds a unique blend of Florida flavors, with specialties from the smoker like a half chicken, pork shoulder, cedar plank salmon ribs, and BBQ cheddar sausage, all served with jalapeño cornbread, coleslaw, and a side. You'll find some interesting sides like tomato and watermelon salad, roasted beets, grilled street corn, sweet potato tots, and BBQ cauliflower with paprika sour cream and candied pepitas. Kids can order chicken tenders, mac and cheese, a smoked pork slider, and a smoked half hen.

The drinks at Polite Pig are unlike anything else you'll find on property—because in addition to the beer, the small batch cocktails listed are all on tap. You can get gin and tonic, sangria, and vodka lemonade right from a tap! You'll also find a quality selection of local beers, some even brewed by Cask and Larder. My favorite is Lone Palm Golden Ale, a blonde-style ale. A portion of this bar is outside, which makes it very convenient to walk up, order a drink, and continue your stroll around Disney Springs.

Sprinkles Cupcakes

DDP: No / Cost: $
TYPE: American; Quick Service; Snacks

There's a cupcake ATM here. Need I say more? Well...there is a bit more to say. A cupcake ATM means that at any time of the day you can swipe your credit card and a cupcake of your choosing pops out. Oh, and the ATM is bright pink. If all you want is a cupcake, this might be a good idea because the line for Sprinkles can get lengthy, especially after the denizens of Disney Springs have had their dinners. In addition to cupcakes, they serve cookies and ice cream. To have the best of both worlds, get the Sprinkles Sandwich—your choice of a Sprinkles cupcake cut in half, and in between the cupcake is a scoop of ice cream. It's decadent and best shared—two desserts in one! You can also order shakes, malts, and floats. Sprinkles is a national franchise with an e-mail rewards program; if you sign up for it, you get a free cupcake on your birthday.

Frontera Cocina

DDP: One credit (T) / Cost: $$ (TiW, lunch only)
TYPE: Mexican; Casual; Lunch and Dinner

Chef Rick Bayless specializes in Mexican cuisine with a twist, and that's what is served here. This airy, bright restaurant is located across the waterway from Morimoto near Sprinkles.

The dinner and lunch menus are identical. To start, you can order guacamole—be sure to tell your server how spicy you like it as they can adjust it based on your taste. For a twist on guacamole, you can also order guacamole with Nueske bacon. Other appetizers include toasted pumpkin seed hummus made with creamy Yucatecan pumpkin seed-habanero dip and crispy cucumber and jicama served with warm tortilla chips. You'll find salads, tacos, and tortas on the menu. For more hearty options, order an entrée like Oaxacan Red Chile Chicken, Creekstone Ribeye Steak (made with crispy onion strings, Cotija mashed potatoes, caramelized plantains with cheese and tomatillo salsa), or carne asada. Kids can order quesadillas, tacos, or enchiladas. For dessert, pick a refreshing sorbet, ancho chile chocolate cake, pecan pie bar, or coconut-lime cuatro leches.

The margaritas here are top-notch, and include Chef Rick's signature Frontera Margarita with Casa Noble blanco tequila, Royal Combier, fresh lime juice, agave nectar, and a salted rim. This is the only other place outside of La Cava del Tequila in Epcot's Mexico Pavilion where you can order the avocado margarita with Casa Noble blanco tequila, melon liqueur, avocado, fresh lime juice, and hibiscus salt rim. If margaritas aren't your style, there are plenty of other cocktails, sangria, wine, and beers available.

Chicken Guy!

DDP: One credit (Q) / Cost: $
TYPE: American; Quick Service; Lunch and Dinner

Chicken Guy! Is one of the newest eateries in Disney Springs. It opened in August 2018 and is the brainchild of Guy Fieri (of *Diners, Drive-Ins, and Dives*, and unnaturally frosted hair-fame) and Robert Earl (of Earl of Sandwich fame). Even though there are a few sandwiches and salads here, this quick-service location is best known for their chicken tenders—and the 22 signature sauces in which you can douse them. Fieri is the "Boss of Sauce," and you can carefully curate your sauce masterpiece using options like bourbon brown sugar barbecue, buttermilk ranch, or the sauce to end all sauces, Guy's signature Donkey Sauce—made with mayo, roasted garlic, mustard, Worcestershire, and lemon. You can choose two sauces to compliment your tender order, which come in servings of three or five. This is a pretty good value for the amount of food you get. You can also order your tenders crispy fried or grilled. No trip to Chicken Guy! is complete without a photo of the cutout of Guy Fieri holding a chicken.

Planet Hollywood Observatory

DDP: One credit (T) / Cost: $$
TYPE: American; Casual; Lunch and Dinner

Guy Fieri strikes again! Past the shopping district, across the way from the Coca-Cola Store Rooftop Beverage Bar near the Lime parking garage, you will find Planet Hollywood Observatory. The original Walt Disney World Planet Hollywood opened at Disney Springs (then Downtown Disney) in 1994. Major renovations were made, and the restaurant was re-themed and re-branded as the Planet Hollywood Observatory in 2017. This restaurant takes the Hollywood-themed memorabilia that Planet Hollywood is known for and melds it with the look of a planetarium. (I never realized how strange that concept sounded until I typed it out.) The food options also got a huge overhaul with the addition of a new menu overseen by polarizing celebrity chef Guy Fieri. If you've been to a Planet Hollywood before, you'll understand the shtick. There are still big portions and a bunch of random Hollywood posters and artifacts on the walls. However, with the new re-theming, the location is somehow louder (both auditorily and visually) than ever before. Contemporary pop and rock music videos are playing and being broadcasted onto the dome ceiling at a volume that is just a bit too loud for my liking. If you prefer your dinner conversations to be nearly drowned out by Better Than Ezra and Smash Mouth songs, then you may enjoy this theming decision, but it certainly isn't for everyone. There is, however, balcony seating with scenic views of Disney Springs that I think is a much more suitable option if it isn't too hot and humid.

The lunch and dinner menus are exactly the same in content and price. The fare is American style, specializing in burgers, nachos, specialty sandwiches, and some seafood and grilled options. They offer menu items that are akin to many other chain restaurants, but they do a great job with their comfort food selections. Appetizers include the Nachos Grande, the World-Famous Chicken Crunch (all-natural chicken tenders hand-breaded with a crunchy sweet coating, served with signature Creole mustard sauce), and the Texas Tostados (crispy gyoza skins topped with BBQ chicken, sautéed onions, blend of cheddar and Monterey Jack cheeses, and drizzled with sour cream and BBQ sauce, served with pico de gallo). Healthier options are available in the form of large entrée salads including a Caesar salad with shrimp and the Steakhouse (superfood blend of kale, julienned broccoli, slivered Brussels sprouts, cabbage and romaine, sliced bistro steak, bacon, bleu cheese crumbles, Parmesan, crispy onion straws, croutons, and Caesar dressing). Featured prominently on the menu are the Guy! Big Bite Burgers as well as the Guy! Signature Sandwiches. The burgers include a Plain Jane Cheeseburger and some interesting concoctions like the award-winning Bacon Mac-n-Cheese burger (with Apple-wood-smoked bacon, six cheese mac-n-cheese, LTOP, crispy onion straws, and donkey sauce on a brioche bun served with triple fries). The signature sandwiches include the Champion-ship Pulled Pork (crisped pulled pork with Guy's signature BBQ sauce, slaw, pickles, crispy onion straws, and Donkey Sauce on a brioche bun served with triple fries) and the Pimento Grilled Cheese (a grilled cheese made with six cheese mac-n-cheese, cheddar and pimento cheese stuffed between two slices of sour-dough bread, and served with triple fries). They also offer some grill specialties like sesame-ginger salmon, BBQ ribs, and a NY strip steak (that serves two).

The menu offers a large wine list from some notable celeb-rity wineries such as the Barrymore Pinot Grigio, Francis Coppola Wizard of Oz Merlot, and the Vanderpump Rosé. Similarly, you have Hollywood-themed signature drinks like the Celebrity Margarita (Cuervo Silver tequila, Grand Marnier, and fresh sour) and Dr. Zhivago's Mule (New Amsterdam vodka, Gosling's ginger beer, and lime juice). Be aware that the Stargazer's Bar attached to the restaurant does not serve food.

Stargazers Bar

DDP: No / Cost: $
TYPE: American; Lounge; Drinks

This is the bar attached to the outside of Planet Hollywood. It's located under the top-floor balcony seating, and is a hidden gem when it comes to craft beer selection. No other spot in Walt Disney World has the wide array of local brew choices that Star-gazers has. There are also domestic bottles available and a wine list, as well as a list of hand-crafted cocktails like the Stargazer

(Stoli Blueberi vodka and lemonade with fresh blueberry and basil), the Observatory (vodka, Limoncino Bottega, peach tea, and prosecco), and the Sparkling Sputnik (prosecco, sparkling water, lime, blueberries, and mint). An interesting fact about the craft beers at Stargazers: you cannot order any of these if you are dining at Planet Hollywood. They are exclusively for guests of Stargazers. Often the lounge and restaurant at a location will share a kitchen and offer comparable food selections, but there is *no food* to be had at Stargazers. It's strictly drinks. Stargazers has one of those few-and-far-between Disney discounts with a daily happy hour from 4–7pm where all of their craft beer pints are $5. I would say that's really out of this world.

West Side

Candy Cauldron

It's clear to me why Snow White couldn't stay away from that apple in the movie. I mean, they look delicious! Even if you aren't hungry (because you may have had a mix of lobster corn dogs, tacos, pizza, and sushi—not judging), it's worth stopping by Candy Cauldron just to watch the magic happen. You are sure to be mesmerized by the show kitchen. Candy Cauldron sells many of the baked good treats you'll see at the Main Street Confectionary in Magic Kingdom, like caramel apples and cupcakes. They also sell the Chip 'n' Dale salty treats, Goofy's candy treats, and bulk candies.

Disney Food Trucks

The Exposition Park area of Disney Springs teems with food trucks. Two food trucks that you'll usually find there are Fantasy Fare and Spring's Streets Tacos. Fantasy Fare's offerings include shrimp and lobster mac and cheese, chicken and waffles, chicken strips, and corn dogs. Spring's Streets has tacos of all varieties: steak, fish, rice and bean, and chicken. You can order all the same or mix-and-match flavors. You'll also find a deceivingly large drink menu, from margaritas to refreshing brews like the 3 Daughters Beach Blonde Ale. This is a great spot to share a snack or get a drink as you meander through Disney Springs.

AMC Theatre Fork & Screen

DDP: No/ Cost: $-$$$
TYPE: American; Casual; Lunch and Dinner

Florida weather can be unpredictable, and if you have a rainy day on your vacation, it's a good thing there's a huge movie theatre in Disney Springs to wait out the storm. The AMC Theatre Fork & Screen affords you the opportunity to buy a ticket to a movie, and then order dinner and drinks while you watch the movie. This isn't your standard popcorn and soda either—you have a sweeping variety of shareable plates, entrées, desserts, and libations. While enjoying the movie, you'll be lounging in plush chairs with your own call button for your server if you want to order anything else.

You can start with shareable bites like nachos, bacon tots, loaded brisket fries, boneless wings, or crispy Brussels sprouts. You can also order the Big Bite Sampler with boneless wings, loaded brisket fries, pretzel bites, and dipping sauces. For heartier options, look for the flatbread, bowl, or burger sections of the menu. Favorites include southern-style chicken tenders, fish and chips, crispy shrimp, a taco trio, and chicken quesadillas. Kids can order burgers, chicken tenders, mac and cheese, and fish and chips. Before the final act concludes, get yourself dessert, like the molten chocolate churros, brownie sundae, or the Oreo milkshake. It will have you wanting to stay for a double feature.

MacGUFFINS

DDP: No/ Cost: $
TYPE: American; Lounge; Snacks, Lunch, and Dinner

MacGUFFINS is the lounge inside the AMC movie theatre. Meet here, before or after a flick, for drinks—or food. They have a great selection of bar food. Think dips and fried foods: loaded potato skins, parmesan fries, queso blanco dip and chips, crab Rangoon dip, and buffalo wings. If you want something more substantial, try one of their specialty burgers like the Blue Max with bleu cheese crumbles and bleu cheese dressing, the Mushroom Swiss with Swiss cheese and sautéed mushrooms, or the Fire Burger with ground beef stuffed with jalapeños and topped with fried jalapeños. Kids can order a quesadilla, chicken tenders, flatbread pizzetta, or grilled cheese. If you're eating at MacGUFFINS, there's a good chance you are waiting to see a movie, so in addition to all the food, you can also order traditional pre-movie snacks like popcorn, M&Ms, Skittles, or Reese's Pieces.

Starbucks

DDP: No/ Cost: $
TYPE: American; Quick Service; Snacks

This location is the same as your neighborhood Starbucks—coffee, frapps, and refreshers. You also can order breakfast sandwiches, wraps, and pastries all day. The Starbucks location in the Marketplace has an identical menu.

Bongos Cuban Café

DDP: One credit (T) / Cost: $$
TYPE: Cuban; Casual; Lunch and Dinner

Gloria and Emilio Estefan opened this restaurant in 1997 to capture the flavor of Old Havana, Cuba. The tropical style is featured in the décor of the restaurant, with bar stools that look like bongo drums, lush greenery, and bright colors—this style is also prevalent in the food.

The lunch and dinner menus are the same. You can add proteins to your garden or Caesar salads like shrimp, chicken breast, the catch of the day, or churrasco (grilled beef). Try the Estefan Kitchen Cuban Combo for a sampler-sized taste of the appetizers: Applewood bacon wrapped maduros (fried plantains), breaded stuffed potatoes, black bean hummus, plantain chips, and ham croquettes. The menu is divided into meats, chicken, and seafood. Carnivores can enjoy the award-winning slow-roasted Cuban pork, which is marinated for 24 hours and topped with grilled onions and rice, or the authentic Cuban churrasco, a 10-oz. Cuban-style steak served with chimichurri sauce. Chicken choices include Miriam's "Special" chicken and rice, roasted chicken, or chicken vaca frita, which is crispy seared shredded chicken marinated with the Estefan Kitchen Cuban Mojo topped with grilled onions, rice, and sweet plantains. Seafood choices include the grilled seafood platter, shrimp with garlic sauce, seafood paella (serves 2), and the Cuban Criollo Seafood Combo with lobster tail, gulf shrimp, sea scallops, black mussels, clams, calamari, and fresh fish. There is also a Triple C Section of the menu (Calorie Conscious Cuban) with a grilled seafood platter, a fresh catch of the day, and Mojo chicken. You'll find flan for dessert as well as chocolate three-milk cake, rice pudding, and guava cheesecake. Kids can order burgers, grilled chicken breast, nuggets, or a palomilla steak.

There are beers, wines, and specialty cocktails. If you are a wine drinker, try the Estefan Kitchen chardonnay or merlot. You could also order the Glorious Cosmopolitan, Gloria Estefan's signature cosmo done the way she likes it: Grey Goose L'Orange Vodka, Cointreau, orange, cranberry and lime juices, with a splash of Sprite. Or, if you want to try Mr. Estefan's favorite mojito, get the Luxury Mojito with Botran Solera Rum aged for up to 18 years. Have a few of these babies and you just might find yourself as the lead in a conga line!

Bongos Cuban Café Express

DDP: No / Cost: $
TYPE: Cuban; Quick Service; Snacks, Lunch, and Dinner

If you don't want the commitment of a sit-down meal at Bongos, go express. The menu has a few small bites like empanadas and the Cuban Party Box with ham croquette, hand-breaded stuffed potato with beef, mini Cuban sandwich, and a guava pastry. You can also get a Cuban sandwich here (you can't get it in the sit-down restaurant)—their classic pressed sandwich made with award-winning slow-roasted pork, ham, pickles, Swiss cheese, and mustard served with French fries. There are other sandwiches and wraps, and two entrées: chicken bites and Cuban criolla beef. Kids can try a mini version of the Cuban sandwich or the midnight sandwich with pork, ham, pickles, Swiss cheese, and mustard, on sweet Cuban bread. The full-sized midnight sandwich can be found on the adult's menu. Wash it down with some Central/South American sodas like Coco Rico, Jupiña, and Inca Cola, or Cuba's own Ironbeer.

House of Blues Restaurant and Bar

DDP: One credit (T) / Cost: $$ (TiW)
TYPE: Southern/American/Global; Casual; Lunch and Dinner

Catch a concert at this lively venue, and stay for the spin on southern food. Lunch and dinner menus are the same. Get the Voodoo shrimp, gumbo, or jalapeño-cheese cornbread to start, then for entrées try shrimp and grits, jambalaya with Cajun shrimp, blackened salmon, or baby back ribs. The burger and sandwich selections are plentiful. There is the signature HOB Burger served on a brioche bun with lettuce, tomato, and onion, with French fries. There's also the Juicy Lucy with beef and bacon, and the BBQ bacon burger with cheddar and Applewood-smoked bacon. Try the New Orleans Muffaletta for a sandwich with Southern flair. There are also family-style platters like the fried chicken dinner and the smokehouse platter to be shared among four people. Kids can choose from the typical fare of pizza, cheeseburgers, a hot dog, pasta, chicken tenders, grilled cheese, and mac and cheese. Desserts include key lime pie, bread pudding, or the Georgia sundae.

The cocktail menu is full of nods to rock songs, like the Midnight Rider (Ole Smoky Apple Pie moonshine, Sailor Jerry spiced rum, sour, and cola), the Beast of Bourbon (Knob Creek bourbon, maple syrup, and chocolate bitters), and the Rock Me Hurricane (Bacardi Superior rum, Bacardi spiced rum, amaretto, orange and pineapple juices, topped with a Bacardi Black rum float). Also, House of Blues has something that not a lot of Disney dining locations have—a discount. They have a true happy hour every day from 11:30am through 5:00pm.

House of Blues hosts a Sunday Gospel Brunch where local talent performs gospel songs. There is an all-you-care-to-enjoy buffet with breakfast items and a carving station. It's the perfect brunch option for big groups. The Gospel Brunch is outside the limits of the Disney reservation system, so you'll have to call the House of Blues box office at 407 934-2583.

The Smokehouse at House of Blues

DDP: No / Cost: $
TYPE: American; Quick Service; Snacks, Lunch and Dinner

Carolina-slow-cooked meats are the name of the game here. This quick-service stop is a dressed-down version of the House of Blues. Entrées include pulled pork sandwiches, pulled chicken sandwiches, smoked turkey legs, smoked brisket sandwiches, baby back ribs, nachos (with or without pulled pork, chicken, or beef brisket), and a hot dog. It wouldn't be truly southern-style without a side of cole slaw or baked beans. Kids can choose a smaller version of the smoked pulled pork slider or a hot dog.

House of Blues, The Front Porch

DDP: No / Cost: $
TYPE: American; Lounge; Snacks, Lunch and Dinner

This outdoor bar is wedged between the restaurant and the concert venues of House of Blues. It's an intimate setting with live entertainment every evening. There is a rotating selection of craft beers as well as some domestics like Dos Equis, Miller Lite, Bud Light, Lagunitas IPA, and Corona. You'll also find a selection of rosé, red, and white wines, along with champagnes.

Splitsville Dining Room

DDP: One credit (T) / Cost: $$ (TiW)
TYPE: American; Casual; Lunch and Dinner

Located near the Orange parking garage, the multi-level Splitsville is half bowling alley, half restaurant, with a retro feel. You could picture the Incredibles knocking down a few pins in this mid-century modern spot. I love Splitsville. I'm usually traveling with a group, and this makes it hard to a) find a reservation that fits everyone and b) find a restaurant that caters to everyone's tastes. When I first saw this menu, I was skeptical. How in the world can a place be good at sushi *and* pizza? Are they valuing quantity over quality? They are not. This is an extensive menu that is sure to please every taste.

You'll see bar fare on their appetizers list like sliders, chicken tenders, fries, and nachos, along with many varieties of pizza: cheese, BBQ chicken, Hawaiian, Firehouse, and Meat Lovers. Splitsville is one of the best places to order sushi in Disney World (second only to Morimoto Asia or maybe Kimonos at the Swan Hotel). Fresh sushi rolls like the California Roll, Ninja Crunch, Super Tuna, Crouching Dragon, and Fantasy Roll are on their sushi list. Their handheld list includes a buffalo chicken sandwich, a foghorn burger with pepper jack cheese and a fried egg, a turkey club supreme, and a BBQ pulled-pork sandwich. While their entrées are eclectic and range from short ribs and mashed potatoes to fish and chips, a lot of them are served bowl or salad style. One of my favorites is the taco bowl with ground beef, black bean-corn salsa, white rice topped with shredded lettuce, pickled jalapeños, cheddar jack cheese, and sour cream in a tortilla bowl. Kids can order burgers, hot dogs, pizza, chicken tenders, grilled cheese, and pasta. Desserts include the Ghirardelli brownie a la mode, cupcakes, Giant Cake (which is a generous portion of the chef's cake of the day featured in their in-house bakery), a Super Sundae, and a root beer float. Be aware that the food portions at Splitsville are large. It's a good place to split(ville) your order.

The lively atmosphere lends itself to having a few adult beverages. There's a bar outside, often with live musicians, serving drafts and bottled beers, wines, bowl drinks, and specialty cocktails. The bowl drinks are 18 ounces, and you have your choice of flavors: Long Island iced tea, Pink Paloma, Blueberry Lemonade, and Hurricane. Looking for a refreshing cocktail? The Watermelon Smash fits the bill: watermelon-infused vodka, muddled with fresh watermelon, lime juice, and simple syrup.

I wouldn't recommend Splitsville to a couple looking to have a romantic dinner. It's loud, well, because it's a bowling alley. But, it's a great place for a family who wants to bowl a few frames and have a good dinner. They have some tables right at the end of the lanes, so you can grab a bite to eat in the middle of a game. Since this restaurant houses a full bowling alley, it's large and can hold a lot of people. You most likely will be able to walk up and get a table without needing an ADR.

Wetzel's Pretzels

DDP: No / Cost: $
TYPE: American; Quick Service; Snacks

This Wetzel's is located near Planet Hollywood and Stargazers Bar. It is identical to the location found in the Marketplace. Take a break from the Disney pretzels shaped like Mickey's head and try one of these, either an original pretzel twist with warm dough and salt, or a bite sized "Bitz." Bitz might be better if you plan on sharing your snack. Both Bitz and pretzels come in pizza, cinnamon, sour cream and onion, and almond crunch flavors. Wetzel's also serves a hot dog wrapped in a pretzel.

YeSake

DDP: No / Cost: $
TYPE: Global; Quick Service; Snacks

This kiosk offers customizable bowls and wraps. Pick your protein from ahi tuna, cooked shrimp, Yakiniku Beef, salmon, and grilled chicken. Then, top it with lettuce, cabbage, cucumber, kale, carrot, spinach, onion, avocado, cheese, pico de gallo, celery, corn chips, sour cream, walnut, potato sticks, or tempura crunch. Finish it off with a sauce and have it wrapped in a flour tortilla or in a bowl. There are an assortment of non-alcoholic slushies like green tea colada, tart citrus cranberry, coconut mango freeze, and strawberry sour. There are also plenty of sake drinks and alcoholic slushies if that's more your speed.

Häagen-Dazs

DDP: No / Cost: $
TYPE: American; Quick Service; Snacks

Beat the heat with one of the shakes, cones, or sundaes that make Häagen-Dazs a household name. Cones come in kiddie sizes and go up to a large. Get a Dazzler Sundae in either the banana split, Rocky Road, Dulce Split, or mint chip varieties. You can get shakes and add toppings—there are many ways to customize your order. For caffeine, get the frozen coffee frappe in coffee, mocha, or caramel flavors.

Joffrey's Handcrafted Smoothies

DDP: No / Cost: $
TYPE: American; Quick Service; Snacks

Rounding out the circle of snacks near Stargazers Bar is Joffrey's Smoothies. Even though the focus of Joffrey's is coffee, this location features handcrafted smoothies. You have your choice of smoothie concoctions like the Purple Piñata (apple juice strawberries, raspberries, blueberries, and yogurt), Flamingo Frost (pineapple juice, strawberries, bananas, and yogurt), and the Razzy Jazzy (cranberry juice, strawberries, raspberries, and yogurt). The menu is the same as the location in the Marketplace.

CHAPTER SEVEN

Disney's Boardwalk

The Boardwalk opened in 1996. Since then, it's grown to be a go-to place for food, drink, and entertainment within walking distance of Hollywood Studios and the International Gateway entrance to Epcot. Disney's Boardwalk was designed to pay homage to the great Eastern boardwalks around the turn-of-the-century like Atlantic City and Coney Island. You'll see stunning Victorian architecture and dazzling lights on the marquee. Since 1996, the Boardwalk area has become somewhat of a Disney Springs lite, boasting spectacular places to eat and drink.

Boardwalk Kiosks, Wagons, and Carts

You'll find a few stands along the boards. Marvelous Joe's Margaritas sells margaritas, piña coladas, and snacks like Mickey pretzels and roasted nuts. You'll also see the Boardwalk pizza window next to Trattoria Al Forno, which sells whole pizzas or slices. This is one of the only places on the Boardwalk that is open late for food. There's a kiosk across from Flying Fish on the water that sells small fried goodies like mozzarella sticks, fried mac and cheese bites, hot dogs, and chicken tenders. You'll also find a stand close to Big River that sells funnel cakes.

AbracadaBar

DDP: No / Cost: $
TYPE: American; Unique/Themed; Drinks

This bar, tucked between Flying Fish and Trattoria Al Forno, puts the magic in Disney magic. It's a very small space with limited indoor seating. If you can get a seat inside—do it! The vanishing libations and standing ovations don't quite have the same effect in the blinding Florida sun.

The menu is drinks only, with a few non-alcoholic options, but no food is served in AbracadaBar. The names of the drinks are a nod to the craft of magic: the Conjurita (El Mayor Tequila, Cointreau, simple syrup, and lime juice), Magic Mirror (Bacardi Rum, soda water, mango syrup, Sprite, and lime juice), and Pepper's Ghost (Ciroc Pineapple vodka and habanero lime). The Seashore Sweet (an homage to this bar's prior tenant) is made with Absolut Cintron, lemonade, and cotton candy syrup. You can request that it be made virgin-style without the vodka.

When AbracadaBar first opened, it was really special—highly themed with an attentive staff. Many of the drinks came with a side of magic, like changing colors, smoke, you name it. Now that they've been open for a few years, some of the pixie dust has faded. The staff is more concerned with churning out guests rather than "wasting time" with the magic tricks. This used to be somewhere I simply had to go during each of my trips, but it isn't anymore.

Ample Hills Creamery

DDP: One credit (S) / Cost: $
TYPE: American; Quick Service; Snacks

When Disney CEO Bob Iger likes your ice cream, big things happen. Just ask Brian Smith, the owner and operator of Ample Hills Creamery, a New York City-based ice cream shop. You can find the only location of Ample Hills outside of the tri-state area right on Disney's Boardwalk thanks to Mr. Iger's love of Ample Hills. This is some of the best ice cream on property, with unique, hand-dipped flavors like Cotton Candy, Coffee Toffee Coffee, and Sally Sells Seashells (marshmallow ice cream with chocolate shells). Nothing complements a stroll down the boardwalk like a hand-dipped cone.

Belle Vue Lounge

DDP: No / Cost: $ (TiW)
TYPE: American; Casual; Breakfast and Drinks

By day, the Belle Vue Lounge is the place you can get coffee and pastries if you're staying at the BoardWalk Inn. By night, it's a bar tucked away from the rest of the crowds of the Boardwalk. This lounge is located on the second floor of the BoardWalk Inn (the lobby level- non-DVC side) with a view of the main lawn. The leather-bound books, old board games, and comfortable couches give you the impression that you've stepped right into the 1930s. The bar and seating area here is small, so it's conducive to talking to strangers. Even though it looks a little stuffy, and you'll see Gatsby-esque drinks like the Sidecar Noir and Tom Collins on the drink menu, this lounge is far from being too pretentious.

Boardwalk Bakery

DDP: One credit (Q) / Cost: $
TYPE: American; Quick Service; Snacks, Breakfast, Lunch, and Dinner

If you stay on Walt Disney World property during your stay, you'll notice that each of the resorts has a cafeteria or counter-service option where you can grab quick bites. This is the Boardwalk's version of that. This eatery is located on the Boardwalk in between the pizza window and Ample Hills Creamery.

For breakfast, order pastries, muffins, and coffee. You can also get your refillable mug replenished here. They recently added a selection of hot breakfast sandwiches to their menu including the Everything Everything Sandwich (everything bagel, fried egg, and Tillamook cheddar cheese), the Butter Butter Sandwich (brioche, shaved ham, scrambled eggs, and buttery fontina cheese spread), and the Ooey Gooey (artisan roll, eggs, cheddar and mozzarella cheese, capicola and tomato). I would venture to say these might be even more desirable than a Mickey waffle.

Lunch and dinner options include sandwiches like the Big and Beefy (focaccia, roast beef, caramelized fennel, onions, and creamy mustard sauce) and the Roasty Toasty (ciabatta, arugula, Portobello mushroom, red onion, zucchini, and sweet red pepper mayo). You can also order a Caesar salad or an herb-grilled chicken and apple mixed greens salad. The Disney Check meal is a turkey sandwich on Goldfish bread. Kids can also order ham and cheese on a bun. Besides what is found on the menu, stop in to see their seasonal cupcake and treat offerings.

Big River Grill and Brewing Works

DDP: No / Cost: $ (TiW)
TYPE: American; Quick Service; Snacks

Located on the Boardwalk in front of Disney' Boardwalk Villas near Jellyrolls piano bar, this microbrewery serves up a wide variety of freshly brewed craft beers as well as pub favorites ranging from southwestern, Cajun, fresh seafood, chicken, and pasta. The restaurant is casual and contemporary with lots of seating at both the bar and tables. Additionally, it showcases floor-to-ceiling glass windows where you can watch the on-site brewmaster working on crafting specialty beers while you enjoy your meal.

Menu items and pricing are the same for both lunch and dinner. Appetizers include pub favorites like Brewery Nachos (tortilla chips with pepper jack cheese, jalapeño, pico de gallo, and sour cream), Asiago, Artichoke, and Crab Dip (topped with pico de gallo and served with toasted crostini), and a chicken quesadilla (filled with shredded chicken, peppers, onions, tomatoes, and pepper jack cheese served with sour cream and guacamole). They offer a decent variety of salads including a Santa Fe Ranch chicken salad as well as the Brewer's Cobb. Also available is either a cup or bowl of their touted Beer Cheese Soup. Sandwiches include the California Chicken (grilled chicken, swiss cheese, guacamole, lettuce, tomato, and chipotle mayonnaise served with kettle chips) and the Brewer's Club (roasted turkey, ham, bacon, cheddar and swiss cheeses, tomato, and lettuce with chipotle mayonnaise and kettle chips). They also offer an assortment of burgers. Main dishes include shrimp scampi pasta (sautéed shrimp with roasted garlic butter, lemon, white wine, and tomatoes over linguine topped with parsley and served with kettle chips), baby back ribs, and blackened Creole salmon (with a creamy Cajun sauce, garlic butter, and green onions served with seasonal vegetables and cilantro-lime rice). Kids' entrées include grilled cheese sandwiches, macaroni & cheese, hot dogs, and hamburgers. Even though this is a brewery, it is still a quiet family-friendly environment, and you will likely see many families with children enjoying a meal here.

It's difficult to provide you with an adequate description of the variety of beers Big River Grille offers, as they are seasonal and constantly rotating. When I last ate here, they had an Irish red ale, a pale ale, and a hefeweizen. If beer isn't your thing, don't fret. They also have a large selection of bottled and individual glasses of wine, as well as traditional cocktails like mojitos, margaritas, and Long Island Iced Teas. If you are looking for a laid-back atmosphere where you can get a good burger or nachos and enjoy some craft beer, you could do a lot worse than Big River Grille and Brewing Works.

ESPN Club

DDP: One credit (T) / Cost: $$ (TiW)
TYPE: American; Unique/Themed; Lunch and Dinner

ESPN Club is located on the last piece of Boardwalk real estate before you get to Epcot. Note that this is an ESPN CLUB and not an ESPN ZONE: you won't find all the bells and whistles of arcade games here. What you will find is TVs—lots of 'em—broadcasting pretty much every sport known to man, woman, or child.

The menu is quintessential bar food: chicken strips, wings, nachos, pretzels, and burgers. A heartier appetite might enjoy an entrée like a pork chop, vegetable lo mein, or white cheddar pasta and cheese. Kids can order Disney Check meals like seasonal grilled fish, turkey pinwheel, or grilled chicken. They can also order a cheeseburger or hot dog. Post-game desserts include s'mores bread pudding, Carolina buttermilk pie, and fruit crisp.

There are a few "Championship Spirits" on the menu like the ESPY (Absolut Mandrin, Peach schnapps, orange and pineapple juices, and Sprite), the Bloody Mulligan, and the MVP Margarita. You'll also see some draft picks like Bud, Coors, Miller, Jai-Alai, and Blue Moon. ESPN Club isn't world renowned for its food, but it's good for enjoying a game with friends and family. My biggest trip of the year is smack dab in the middle of college football season, and this is the spot where my Penn State-fan friends would plant themselves to watch the game—then head into Epcot for the Food and Wine Festival, of course.

Flying Fish

DDP: Two credits (T) / Cost: $$$-$$$$ (TiW)
TYPE: Seafood/American; Fine/Signature; Dinner

For a complete review, see the entry under "BoardWalk Inn" in the next chapter.

Trattoria Al Forno

DDP: One credit (T) / Cost: $$ (TiW)
TYPE: Italian; Casual; Breakfast and Dinner

Located at the spot that was once home to Cat Cora's Kouzzina, Trattoria Al Forno opened in late 2014. The cuisine is Old World, rustic Italian in a casual atmosphere. This restaurant is a great choice if you can't get any dining reservations in Epcot, because it's only steps away from the International Gateway.

For breakfast, Trattoria Al Forno is home to one of Walt Disney World's newest character dining experiences. Join power couples Ariel and Prince Eric from *The Little Mermaid* and Rapunzel with Flynn Rider from *Tangled* for breakfast. Breakfast is prix fixe. You start with pastries for everyone to share, then you have the choice of a starter—either fruit salad or a berry, yogurt, and granola parfait. Choose one of the following entrées: King Triton's Shipwreck al Forno (calzone with eggs, bell peppers, salami, bacon, sausage, cheese, and gravy), Two-Eggs Poached Underwater (fennel sausage, gravy, and parmesan cheese over polenta with toasted focaccia), Royale Breakfast (oak-grilled steak, cheesy-egg torte, fonduta with breakfast potatoes and crispy onions), Golden Frittata, Tangled Eggs, Tower of Pancakes, and Swimmers Delight (egg white omelet with smoked salmon, goat cheese, spinach, mushroom, and tomato with breakfast potatoes). Disney Check meals are smaller versions of the Royale Breakfast and Swimmers Delight. Kids can also order Flounder's Flapjacks (with bacon or sausage) and waffles. Adults can order sangria, peach bellinis, Caprese Bloody Marys, mimosas, and Italian iced coffee.

Trattoria Al Forno reopens at dinnertime without the Disney characters. The antipasti options are calamari, gnocchi, salad, Venetian Mussels, and a salad with mozzarella, tomatoes, and aged balsamic. There are also pizzas on the menu—try the rotating chef's specialty, the vegetarian, or the margherita. Traditional pasta dishes like lasagna, pasta bolognese, chicken parmesan, and ravioli are also available. Enhance any of your dinner choices with a 6-oz strip steak, shrimp, chicken breast, or scallops. Disney Check choices are seasonal fish and chicken breast. Kids can also order pasta with meatballs, strip steak, and pizza. Desserts include tiramisu, gelato, zeppoli, and dark chocolate semolina torta. Order a unique nightcap like the Italian Manhattan, Sicilian Iced Tea, or the Molto Bello (a margarita with a twist). There are also several beer and wine selections to choose from.

CHAPTER EIGHT

Disney Resort Hotels

In this chapter I'll look at not *every* eatery at *every* Disney resort hotel, but rather the unique and signature dining experiences, the dinner shows, and the characters buffets.

Animal Kingdom Lodge

Boma

DDP: One credit (T) / Cost: $$ (TiW)
TYPE: African; Unique/Themed; Breakfast and Dinner

Boma offers a family-style buffet for both breakfast and dinner. They tout savory dishes from numerous African countries as well as some American favorites. The word "Boma" loosely translates to a fence made of sticks which represents an open and natural space for a safe and sheltered environment. This theme is present throughout the dining area with decorative fence-like borders that separate the buffet from the dining area with its thatched roofs and near African-style art and sculptures. Unlike a lot of the other buffet offerings at Disney, you will not find any costumed characters here. The main focus is food, and there is an abundance of it at both breakfast and dinner.

Let's start with the breakfast offerings. Appetizers include a spinach-quinoa salad, cheese selection, smoked salmon, and African fruit fool. No, I'm not insulting you. A "fool" is a mixture of fruit and custard or whipped cream. Entrées include traditional American breakfast items like waffles, omelets, pancakes, and oatmeal. Boma also offers sweet plantains, French toast bread pudding, oak-grilled asparagus and tomatoes, quinoa, and hand-carved turkey. Drinks include assorted juices, milk, coffee, hot tea, and a coconut elixir (ZICO coconut water with pineapple and cranberry juices).

The dinner buffet is extensive. You may be a bit overwhelmed at first with the sheer number of items offered. They have a rotation of soups and stews that include butternut squash soup, Ghanian oxtail stew, spicy Nigerian peanut soup, mulligatawny, and chicken-corn chowder. A plethora of salad options are available including pasta salad, lentil and hearts of palm salad, Tunisian couscous salad, kool slaai, apple jicama salad, as well as chermoula-chilled shrimp salad. Entrées and sides, like the soup offerings, also are run on a rotation. You won't necessarily see the same food options each time you visit. Entrées include pork shoulder, whole roasted salmon, fufu, bobotie, roasted turkey, and spice-crusted beef sirloin, whereas sides could be anything from couscous, peanut rice, and plantain crisps to mashed potatoes and zulu cabbage. Dessert options include key lime cheesecake, apple cobbler, Kenyan coffee tarts, and guava panna cotta. For kids, they also offer chicken bites, mac & cheese, mealie dogs, and penne pasta. You can opt to pay extra for a specialty wine flight or a Boma signature beverages like the Mt. Kilamarita (their ultimate African margarita with Patrón Silver tequila, Van der Hum tangerine liqueur, and sweet-and-sour with a splash of cranberry juice).

If you're looking for an adventurous dining experience or are just aching to try something new, Boma is an excellent spot for both breakfast and dinner. The pickier eaters in your party should be able to find some familiar American food so that everyone can have a meal they truly enjoy.

Jiko

DDP: Two credits (T) / Cost: $$$-$$$$ (TiW)
TYPE: Indian/Mediterranean/African; Fine/Signature; Dinner

Jiko serves as the top-tier signature dining experience at Animal Kingdom Lodge. "Jiko" loosely translated in Swahili means "a cooking place." Only open for dinner, Jiko offers a vibrant mix of African, Indian, and Mediterranean flavors. You'll notice immediately upon entering Jiko that their wine selections are given a front-and-center priority boasting the largest variety of African wines in the United States. The interior design is a beautiful mix of elegance and natural African aesthetic with sculptures of birds appearing to fly overhead in the main dining area and wooden floors with inlay patterns of wheat sheaths representing the importance of harvest. Additionally, you'll find twin wood-burning ovens crackling and a view of the open show kitchen where you can watch the chefs preparing delicious appetizers.

Appetizers at Jiko include North African spiced scallops (with herb chermoula and curried feta crumbles), Bains whiskey-infused watermelon salad (feta powder, candied kumquat, fig-port vinaigrette, rocket, and house-made duck biltong), and the Jiko salad (greens from Epcot's Land Pavilion, stone fruit, pistachio halva, grilled halloumi cheese, and apricot-ginger dressing). Also offered is an artisanal cheese selection as well as a variety of starting dishes "from the cooking place" (prepared by the chefs in the wood-burning ovens). These include an elk confit flatbread (elk loin, harissa-infused goat cheese, olive-arugula salad) and the Taste of Africa (African-inspired dips, pappadum, sesame fatir, and house-made flax seed naan). Entrées include the Mrouzia-style Moroccan lamb tagine (with parsnip silk, roots spinach, medjool date smoor, pomegranate glaze), Snake River Farms Wagyu strip loin (macaroni and cheese, kachumbari, brussels sprouts, South African red wine sauce), and the chermoula chicken (with baba ganoush, fregula salad, and baby squash). You can add enhancements to any entrée, including the Egyptian kushari, coconut-curry shrimp, and Zulu-style sap and beans. Their unique desserts include the Kilimanjaro (Tanzanian chocolate mousse, pistachio financier, pink peppercorn meringue, cacao nib crunch, ras el hanout pineapples) and the Safari Sunset (carrot cake, cornbread calamansi, lemon crémeux, Kenyan coffee streusel, citrus gel, Valrhona dulcey mousse, and candied carrots). Kids' meals include your traditional mac & cheese and cheese pizza. Kids' disney check meals include the market-fresh fish, shrimp with kushari, and grilled chicken breast.

I mentioned the importance of wine at Jiko. Every Wednesday, Jiko hosts a wine tasting from 3pm to 4pm. A sample of flavors from a trio of wines is chosen by the Jiko sommeliers. These wines are paired with a delicious selection of cheeses. For the wine lover in your life, this is an event that is sure to please. As with most signature dining experiences, both the dinner and wine tasting require that guests adhere to the minimum dress code requirements: khakis or slacks for men, and Capri pants, skirts, or dresses for women. With beautiful décor and a menu that is constantly evolving, Jiko is a signature Disney dining experience that the foodie in your life will not want to miss.

Sanaa
DDP: One credit (T) / Cost: $$ (TiW)
TYPE: African/Indian; Unique/Themed; Breakfast, Lunch, Dinner

Head downstairs from the lobby of Animal Kingdom Lodge's Kidani Village to the bottom floor to reach Sanaa. Described on the Disney website as a place to "experience the art of African cooking with Indian flavors," this is a wonderful sit-down restaurant with some of the more unique offerings you'll find dining at Walt Disney World. The word "sanaa" is taken from the Swahili word for "art" and is quite appropriate when you see the vast amount of detail and artistry that has gone into the theming for the restaurant. Matching the beautiful African tapestry of the rest of Kidani Village, Sanaa features handmade African-style art, and you'll even find African proverbs on the walls in certain areas of the restaurant. The main dining area is one of my favorites with faux forestry making it look like you are dining under a lush wooded canopy with decorative hanging lanterns overhead. Oh, and did I mention that views from the dining area overlook the Sunset Savanna? Ask for a window-side table to get the best possible view of the animals as you enjoy your meal. The menu offers a mixture of East African and Indian cuisine and is open for breakfast, lunch, and dinner.

Appetizer and entrée offerings vary across the lunch and dinner menus with some of the favorites carrying over to both. One of the most, if not the most, popular items on the menu is an appetizer that you can find at both lunch and dinner times, the Indian-Style Bread Service. This dish comes in two varieties. The first is where you choose one of the five types of bread to pair with three out of the nine accompaniments. However, for just three dollars more, you get all five types of bread and all nine accompaniments to try. I recommend spending the extra three dollars for a truly delicious and unique experience. You will receive five different types of breads including naan, onion kucha, and paneer paratha. The nine accompaniments with which you can top your bread choice are arranged on a decorative plate in order of most tame to spiciest. This is a fairly large portion and quite possibly one of the most fun dining activities you can have with a family or group of friends while trying all the different flavors and discussing which one is your favorite. Also offered for both lunch and dinner are seasonal soups and a salad sampler.

Lunch entrées include the Sanaa Burger (with spiced mustard and peppadew-goat cheese served with Sanaa chips and pickle spear) and the Kenya Coffee Barbecue Sandwich (pulled pork with root vegetable slaw in a bread bowl served with Sanaa chips and pickle spear). You'll find that dinner entrées are more formal and a bit more expensive than what you'll find on the lunch menu. They include the Berbere-braised lamb shank (served with krummelpap and summer garden chakalaka), the sustainable fish of the day, and African-inspired biryani with chicken (fragrant rice with seasonal vegetables influenced from the Cape of Good Hope). Less adventurous eaters will be happy to know that a grilled New York strip steak is also on the menu. Unique and African-inspired dessert offerings include the Caramel N'dizi (banana financier with caramelized milk chocolate crémeux, hazelnut crunch, banana-white chocolate chantilly, and ginger raspberries) and the Kenyan Coffee Petit Entremet (Kenyan coffee-chocolate mousse, espresso financier, vanilla crémeux, caramel, and Kenyan coffee crumble). Kid's meals are advertised as Create-Your-Own entrées where they choose a main dish like butter chicken, cheese pizza, or a cheeseburger, then select two from the many side selections including citrus-ginger broccolini, seasonal vegetables, fruit cup, or cheddar mac & cheese.

Sanaa offers many unique cocktail creations including the African Starr Mojito (Starr African rum, Van der Hum tangerine liqueur from South Africa, fresh lime juice, and mint) and the Painted Lemur (Amarula fruit cream liqueur and Van der

Hum tangerine liqueur from South Africa combined in a chocolate-striped glass inspired by the distinctive striped tail of the Madagascar lemur). You will also find domestic and imported beers including Tusker Premium Lager from Kenya as well as the Safar Amber Draft (found exclusively throughout Disney's Animal Kingdom). Overall, if you are looking for a truly special experience or looking to try some new and delicious food, Sanaa is a true gem when dining at Walt Disney World.

Beach Club Resort and Villas

Cape May Café
DDP: Two credits (T) / Cost: $$ (TiW)
TYPE: American; Character Buffet; Breakfast
CHARACTERS: Donald, Goofy, Minnie- in beach attire

Cape May Café is character dining in the morning and seafood buffet in the evening sans characters. Even though it's not served at breakfast, the smell of peel-and-eat shrimp permeates the carpet of Cape May Café. Yum.

The breakfast buffet consists of yogurt, fruit, eggs, chorizo, bacon, sausage, home fries, French toast with caramelized bananas, carved ham, bagels, and pastries with whipped cream and strawberry sauce. There is a kid's station with Mickey waffles and assorted cereals.

Character dining outside the Magic Kingdom park and resort area is often overlooked. You might stand a better chance getting a reservation here versus the often packed-to-capacity Chef Mickey's. Cape May Café is a little less loud than Chef Mickey's, but keep in mind you don't get to meet Mickey here. This could be a good option for breakfast before a day in Epcot or even Hollywood Studios.

BoardWalk Inn

Flying Fish
DDP: Two credits (T) / Cost: $$$-$$$$ (TiW)
TYPE: Seafood/American; Fine/Signature; Dinner

At Disney's Boardwalk, right next to AbracadaBar, you'll find the Flying Fish, an outstanding restaurant offering premium seafood and prime steaks. A popular spot since its opening,

Flying Fish received a fresh refurbishment and name change (having previously been called Flying Fish Café) in 2016. Once having carnival-themed décor, the 2016 makeover went in a completely different direction with a focus on elegance now showcasing beautiful chandeliers, tilework, and a fully renovated bar. Still present is a staple of the restaurant, its open kitchen where you can watch the fresh food being prepared by the head chef as well as the other members of the kitchen staff. To take full advantage of this, request Chef's Counter seating. It should be noted that this is one of the few Walt Disney World restaurants with a dress code.. Men are recommended to wear khakis, slacks, or dress shorts, as well as a collared shirt. Women must wear Capri pants, skirts, dresses, or dress shorts.

Flying Fish is only open for dinner and focuses on, you guessed it, seafood dishes. Appetizers include lobster bisque, Prince Edward Island mussels, crispy oysters, and Wisconsin burrata (with masumoto peaches and blueberry-lavender vinaigrette). Entrées include sea bass (with leek fondue, cassis-red wine reduction), savory shrimp pasta (saffron-tomato sauce, garden herbs), oak-grilled salmon (with golden cauliflower silk, beets, and Sicilian pistachios) and Wagyu filet mignon (with vegetable mélange and savory potato beurre blanc). You can add scampi-style sustainable shrimp, Hokkaido scallops, or a cold-water lobster tail to any entrée. Kids' Disney Check meals include sustainable fish, Mickey pasta, and chicken breast. Also for kids, there's "flying" fish and chips and grilled beef strip loin. Dessert options include the Panna "Carpa" (buttermilk panna cotta, strawberry-lime consommé, basil sugar), the Cocoa Breach (chocolate-hazelnut cake, warm ganache), and the Blueberries, Limes, and Sea Shells (mascarpone cream, blueberry-lime compote, hibiscus meringue, and rye bourbon caramel).

The restaurant's 2016 renovation included what Disney describes as new high-tech wine technology which allows more special wines by the ounce. They offer a huge selection of wines as well as a revamped cocktail menu. Dinner is on the expensive side, but those looking for an elegant or romantic dining experience or those looking for a high-quality seafood meal would love Flying Fish.

Contemporary Resort

California Grill

DDP: Two credits (T) / Cost: $$$-$$$$ (TiW)

TYPE: American/Seafood/Sushi; Fine/Signature; Brunch and Dinner

Located on the 15th floor of Disney's Contemporary Resort, California Grill offers a high-class dining experience with panoramic views of the Magic Kingdom and Seven Seas Lagoon. When the Contemporary opened in 1971, the restaurant in this location was called the Top of the World until it was replaced by California Grill in 1995. California Grill underwent a fairly major reimagining in 2013. Through its many incarnations, it has always been a staple of fine dining at Walt Disney World. The current restaurant is themed lavishly in the style of mid-century modern California. With huge windows offering one of the best views on property and an extensive onstage kitchen and sushi bar, the location creates a beautiful ambiance for its delectable menu offerings.

California Grill is only open for dinner and Sunday brunch. As one of the more expensive menus at Disney World, dinner is often best reserved for special occasions or as a "splurge" meal. As expected, menu items are American fare with a focus on California. Appetizers include the Prince Edward Island mussels and frites (with salsa verde butter, cipollini onion, tomato confit, cilantro pesto, and chili-honey aïoli) and Sonoma goat cheese ravioli (with tomato-fennel broth, crispy mushrooms, tiny basil, and arbequina organic olive oil). They also offer a rotating seasonal, handcrafted charcuterie plate as well as a seasonal selection of farmhouse and artisanal Cheeses. In addition to their appetizers, they have a variety of artisanal hand-formed wood-oven pizzas including pepperoni, the Chef's Garden Heirloom Tomato and the Farmer (house-cured pancetta, roasted garlic, sweet onion-olive agrodolce, soft-cooked egg, arugula, and aged pecorino). Hand-rolled sushi rolls are available, from a simple tuna or salmon sashimi to specialty rolls like the New Moon Roll (Maine lobster, avocado, barbecue eel, rice pearls, and gochujang dragon sauce).

Entrées include a variety of delectable dishes such as oak-fired filet of beef (served with fried herb gnocchi, tomato-piquillo jam, smoky pickled pearl onion, and blood orange butter), black grouper (with herb basmati rice, cashew chutney, bok choy, baby shiitake, rock shrimp, and kaffir lime-coconut nage), and seafood spaghetti (with Key West shrimp, Cedar Key clams, mussels, octopus, charred fennel, and lobster broth). Be sure to save room for dessert, as some of the highlights of the menu are of the sweet variety. Some of my favorite items include the s'mores bomboloni (banana jam, house-made graham crackers, and toasted marshmallow ice cream) and the chocolate-cherry pistachio sundae (bing cherry ice cream, house-made waffle shell, Valrhona brownie, warm cherry compote, and pistachios). California Grill also has a fully-featured kids menus with appetizers, entrées (pizza or mac and cheese), Disney Check meals (chicken breast, wild salmon, grilled beef tenderloin), and desserts (seasonal fruit kebobs, puffed rice sushi).

The bar options obviously showcase a number of Napa Valley wines as well as California-brewed beers and ciders. They also offer several non-California and international craft brews in addition to your usual domestic and import beers like Bud Light and Heineken. The bar offers some excellent signature cocktails such as the Anaheim Mule (Hangar 1 Mandarin Blossom Vodka and Fever-Tree Premium Ginger Beer with a splash of orange juice) and the Santa Monica Cider (Rekorderlig Strawberry-Lime Cider, Hendrick's Gin with agave nectar, lime juice, and micro basil).

One of the best parts of eating at the California Grill is the access to the observation deck to watch the fireworks spectacular Happily Ever After at Magic Kingdom. They will pipe in the park music for an extra-special experience.

California Grill's Sunday Brunch is an amazing, albeit expensive, experience. The brunch is an all-you-care-to-enjoy buffet/table-service hybrid offering self-serve selections like house-made charcuterie, bacon and egg salad, deviled eggs, apple salad, and soba noodle salad. Entrées include anything from buttermilk pancakes and eggs benedict to grilled hanger steak (with two eggs any-style, chimichurri, marble potato hash, and charred red onion). Your meal starts with a complimentary mimosa or a specialty non-alcoholic beverage. It is important to note that your mimosas are of the bottomless variety, so drink up. There is also a Bloody Mary bar available for an additional charge. If you hold on to your brunch receipt and bring it to the second-floor check-in podium that night, they will let you on the observation deck to watch the Magic Kingdom fireworks show that night as well. You can also watch the fireworks on the observation deck if you have an earlier dinner reservation—just show your receipt at the host stand.

Chef Mickey's

DDP: One credit (T) / Cost: $$$ (TiW)
TYPE: American; Character Buffet; Breakfast, Brunch, and Dinner
CHARACTERS: Donald, Goofy, Mickey, Minnie, Pluto

Chef Mickey's might be the hottest ticket for character dining on Walt Disney World property. It's located in the Grand Canyon Concourse of the Contemporary—the huge glass atrium through which the monorail passes. At Chef Mickey's, you'll meet the Fab Five (Mickey, Minnie, Donald, Goofy, and Pluto). The atmosphere is loud and lively, and you'll be encouraged to twirl your napkins in the air when the characters parade around the restaurant. As with the other character dining options on property, you get quite a bit of quality face-time with each of the characters. Because of its location in the Contemporary, it's easy to find transportation to or from the Magic Kingdom.

The breakfast buffet consists of seasonal melons and fruits, smoked salmon, quinoa, yogurt, carved ham, breakfast potatoes, bacon, biscuits and gravy, pancakes, and a waffle bar. Kids can enjoy their own section of the buffet with eggs, cereals, and sausage links. To end your breakfast with something sweet, check out the danishes, turnovers, crisped rice treats, muffins, and doughnut holes.

Chef Mickey's has a daily brunch option with breakfast favorites like eggs, breakfast potatoes, bacon, biscuits, gravy, and waffles, and combines it with some of the best dinner items like chili-cornbread casserole, shrimp cocktail, soup, pot roast, baked salmon, and carved pork tenderloin. This is your best bet if you have people in your party who like a heartier breakfast along with people who want to skip right to lunch.

Starters for dinner consist of salad, shrimp cocktail, charcuterie, and fruit salad. The main courses are prime rib at a carving station, roasted chicken, glazed salmon, pot stickers, seafood paella, daily soup and pasta selections, vegetables, pot roast, and smashed potatoes. The kids, or "Mouseketeer," section of the buffet has mac and cheese, tater bite potatoes, steamed broccoli, and chicken nuggets. The dessert buffet has a selection of mousse domes, bread pudding, cheesecake tarts, macarons, and a create-your-own-sundae station with chocolate and vanilla soft-serve.

The cocktail menu at dinner serves a lot of the Disney drinks you'll find all over property, like the Magical Star Cocktail, Beso Del Sol Red Sangria, Captain's Mai Tai, and the Pina Colava.

While the food itself might not be anything to write home about, Chef's Mickeys is located in one of the most iconic Disney World spots, and you'll be meeting the most iconic Disney characters. This makes it a favorite for families and a hot-ticket reservation. If you want to eat here, plan ahead!

The Wave...of American Flavors

DDP: One credit (T) / Cost: $-$$ (TiW)
TYPE: American; Unique/Themed; Breakfast (Buffet), Lunch, Dinner

On the first floor of Disney's Contemporary Resort, tucked away in the northeast corner, you will find the Wave. The restaurant certainly fits the overall theme of the resort with its contemporary and geometric design choices. Right from the start, you walk through a hallway with arched metal sculptures to reach the host stand. There is a large, elegant dining area as well as a stylish lounge. The menu is mostly American fare focusing on farm-to-table ideals using organic and local ingredients. Additionally, this table-service restaurant offers some of the freshest and healthiest options on Walt Disney World property.

There are some overlapping items in both content and price on the lunch and dinner menus, especially when it comes to appetizers, desserts, and cocktails. However, entrées for lunch and dinner are nearly entirely different which provides for a nice variety and warrants multiple visits. Options for starters include lump crab cakes (with Old Bay rémoulade with corn slaw), Prince

Edward mussels (in chardonnay broth with fine herbs, garlic butter, and grilled focaccia), and seasonal soup or salad. Spice-crusted ahi tuna (coconut panna cotta, pineapple-browned butter, cilantro emulsion, shaved radish) is offered as a lunch-exclusive appetizer. Interestingly, you can find a bacon and eggs appetizer (maple-lacquered pork belly with perfect egg and Tillamook smoked cheddar grits) exclusively on the dinner menu.

Lunch entrées include a reuben sandwich (with swiss cheese, sauerkraut, on sunflower seed bread), a noodle bowl (sweet chili bean curd, stir-fried vegetables, udon noodles, and mushroom-dashi broth), and the soup, salad, sandwich which comes with a cup of soup, seasonal salad, and a turkey sandwich. The dinner menu entrées are more refined and quite a bit more expensive. Choices include grilled beef tenderloin (with potato gratin, jumbo asparagus, and red wine reduction), cioppino (sustainable fish, scallop, shrimp, mussels, spiced tomato-clam broth), and seared potato gnocchi (forest mushrooms, sweet potatoes, rainbow swiss chard, and brown butter-parmesan-sage cream). There are also additional allergy-friendly offerings available upon request. Desserts options are the same in offerings and price for both lunch and dinner. Options include a trio of sorbet, artisanal cheese selection, and crème brûlée (vanilla crème brûlée with fresh berries, a no-sugar-added dessert). Kids meals include a cheeseburger, grilled beef kabobs, and a grilled cheese sandwich. Kids' Disney Check Meals include the grilled fish of the day, penne pasta, and grilled chicken breast.

The Wave has a large selection of both alcoholic and non-alcoholic beverages. They offer a variety of healthy smoothies as well as sustainable coffee drinks. Specialty cocktails include the Seven Seas Lagoon Shared Cocktail (Skyy Vodka, Parrot Bay Coconut Rum, blue curaçao, lime, pineapple, fruit boba, and gummy fish) and the Godiva Chocolate Martini (Godiva chocolate liqueur, Stoli Vanil Vodka, white crème de cacao, and Frangelico). They also offer a selection of local, organic craft beers from breweries like Florida Beer Co. and Bold City Brewery.

The Wave is also open for breakfast daily. They offer both a full-service breakfast buffet as well as an à la carte menu that includes breakfast favorites like eggs benedict, omelet your way, and the Wave signature sweet potato pancakes (served with pecan-honey butter and choice of bacon, pork sausage, or chicken sausage). Libations like the Bay Lake Bloody Mary and mimosas (in both the stand-alone and refillable variety) are available. The Wave is an excellent place to eat, especially if you, or the people you are dining with, are looking for more organic or health-conscious food items.

Coronado Springs Resort

Maya Grill
DDP: One credit (T) / Cost: $-$$ (TiW)
TYPE: Mexican/American; Unique/Themed; Dinner

The Maya Grill menu is Mexican/American. Starters include queso fundido, fried calamari, guacamole, and green tortilla soup. Main courses range from the Mexican-inspired Yucatan Roasted Pork (with orange achiote, pickled red onion, guacamole, chilaquiles verde, and corn tortillas), to the traditionally American New York strip. You can also find ribs, tacos, red snapper, and a fajita skillet. Seasonal signatures include a seafood grill platter, a hand-cut bone-in ribeye, and a Parrillada "Del Grill" which includes marinated New York strip, chorizo, and chicken al pastor with bell peppers and grilled onions. Kids can order mac and cheese, tacos, the catch of the day, chicken tenders, seasoned steak in a flour tortilla, grilled chicken breast, or a quesadilla. Desserts are flan, chocolate panna cotta, ancho chili crème brûlée, and sorbet. You'll see a few wines on the menu, but the highlight of the alcoholic selections is the extensive margarita menu. Try the classic margarita or the more out-of-the-box flavors like horchata, jalapeño, or mango blueberry basil. If you simply can't choose, pick the margarita flight—you'll get the mango blueberry basil, classic, horchata, pineapple, and jalapeño flavors in 5 small shot glasses.

Fort Wilderness Resort

Hoop-De-Doo Musical Revue Dinner Show
DDP: Two credits (T) / Cost: $$$-$$$$ (TiW, 9:30 p.m. show only)
TYPE: Country/American; Dinner Show; Dinner

Tucked away in the Campsites, you'll find this high-spirited hootenanny of a dinner show. The show itself is a western-themed vaudeville experience that veteran Disney fans may compare to the old Golden Horseshoe Revue that once ran at Disneyland. The Pioneer Hall Players sing, dance, and provide a hilarious experience that the whole family can enjoy. There is also a decent amount of audience participation (if you so choose). Hoop-De-Doo typically does three shows daily at 4:00pm, 6:15pm, and 8:30pm. There are three categories of seating with a tiered pricing structure, and tickets must be purchased in advance. You also have to plan your trip here wisely. The Disney busses drop off at the main parking lot and you will then have to get a satellite bus to take you to Pioneer Hall.

Dinner is served family-style with all-you-care-to-enjoy fresh baked bread, tossed green salad, baked beans, homestyle fried chicken, smoked BBQ pork ribs, corn-on-the-cob, and strawberry shortcake for dessert. Also included is unlimited soft drinks, coffee, tea, milk, beer, wine, and sangria. That's right, folks. For two full hours, all-you-can-drink beer, wine, and sangria. What a deal! It should be said that you are getting the best of both worlds at Hoop-Dee-Doo. The show itself is top-notch, and the food is delicious. It's soul food done right, and you may have a hard time telling the wait staff "no" when they come around with more delicious treats. Since launching in September 1974, the Hoop-Dee-Doo Musical Revue has been entertaining and providing guests with delicious food. It's no wonder why it's one the country's longest-running dinner shows with over 38,000 performances since its inception.

Grand Floridian Resort & Spa

1900 Park Fare
DDP: One credit (T) / Cost: $$ (TiW)
TYPE: American; Character Buffet; Breakfast, Brunch, and Dinner
CHARACTERS (breakfast and brunch): Mary Poppins, Winnie the Pooh, Tigger, Alice and Mad Hatter
CHARACTERS (dinner): Cinderella, the Prince, Lady Tremaine, Anastasia, and Drizella

When you step into the Grand Floridian, you take on a sense of elegance and class no matter your age, and so this character dining skews more toward the princess-obsessed (yes, I realize that Mary Poppins and Alice aren't princesses, but they are both fabulous). You'll also get a chance to meet some villains. Anastasia and Drizella might be evil, but they are also fun. The dining room is big and bright with a large organ overhead pumping out tunes periodically. It's on the monorail loop which makes touring at the Magic Kingdom easily accessible.

For breakfast, dine on fruit, sticky buns, breads, jams, the famous Floridian strawberry soup, salmon, cheese blintz, potato salad, made-to-order omelets and eggs, ham at a carving station, pancakes, French toast, bacon, sausage, biscuits and gravy. There is a kid's buffet with Mickey waffles, scrambled eggs, sausage, potato puffs, breakfast pastries, and bacon.

While brunching, you get the best of both worlds with the made-to-order omelets and eggs, but also more lunch-y items like tomato mozzarella salad, soup, grits, and peel-and-eat shrimp. You'll also get the fruit and bread selections you find during breakfast. The kid's buffet has Mickey waffles, eggs benedict, buttered corn, scrambled eggs, mac and cheese, and chicken nuggets. Bread pudding and chocolate mousse are dessert options for everyone.

Dinner starters include salads made of greens, fruit, broccoli, potato, and heirloom tomato. Chef's favorites include Floridian strawberry soup, Mississippi catfish, Mongolian beef, curried chicken, honey-sriracha salmon, and the chef's catch of the day. Other savory dishes to be enjoyed on the buffet are jasmine rice, mashed potatoes, claw chowder, vegetables, butternut squash ravioli, peel-and-eat shrimp, pork masala, chicken noodle soup, steamed mussels, and cheese tortellini. There is also a carving station with herb-crusted rib-eye. The kids buffet has macaroni and cheese, hot dogs, chicken nuggets, pasta with olive oil, pizza, and corn. To end your meal, there are many bite-sized desserts that are made in-house. This buffet is practically perfect in every way!

Victoria & Albert's
DDP: No / Cost: $$$-$$$$
TYPE: Modern/American; Fine/Signature; Dinner
The finest of fine dining in all of Disney, Victoria & Albert's is a high-end dining experience for only the most distinguished

of palates. Recipient of the highly coveted AAA Five Diamonds award since 2000, Victoria & Albert's serves up haute American cuisine in an opulent Victorian setting alongside impeccable service. With prix-fixe pricing starting at $185.00 per person (before tax, alcohol, and gratuity), this is a meal typically reserved for a romantic outing or the most special of occasions. There is a strict dress code here as men must wear dinner jackets with dress pants or slacks and dress shoes. Women must wear a cocktail dress, dressy pant suit, or a skirt with a nice blouse. Jeans, shorts, capri pants, sandals, flip-flops, and tennis shoes are not permitted. You can dine in the main dining area or, for an additional cost, in the elegant and private dining space known as Queen Victoria's Room. The Chef's Tasting Menu is seasonal and changes regularly. Check on the Victoria & Albert's website to get the most up-to-date menu.

The meal consists of at least seven customizable courses as well as a dessert course with optional additions and courses to suit your needs. The first course always consists of an amuse-bouche, a single bite-sized hors d'œuvre. At press time, it's a New Zealand langoustine with imperial caviar, avocado, and lime nuage. You are able to add first-course enhancements like the Galilee Osetra caviar or Tagliatelle pasta with Italian white truffles. The second course presently consists of Alaskan King Crab (with sun-kissed melons and pink peppercorn yogurt). Third course is a Virginia black bass (with poppy seed and lemon ravioli). Fourth course consists of a Dover sole with petite squash and tomato water. Fifth course is a roasted French quail with corn pudding and spinach. You're also served a selection of artisanal cheeses from the market, and dessert consists of a bittersweet chocolate dome on praline crunch. There is always a chef's vegetarian tasting menu to choose from as well.

Receiving the "Best of Award of Excellence" by *Wine Spectator*, Victoria & Albert's offers over 600 selections and over 4,200 bottles of eclectic and world-renowned wine tastings. Staff sommeliers are there to regale you in the story of the wines and their regions of origin. Victoria & Albert's is best described as more than just a restaurant but more of an experience. This is one of the most in-demand reservations that must be snagged far in advance, especially if you intend on dining in Queen Victoria's Room. You'll dine amongst the most elegant of décor while dulcet harp music plays. You'll have two dedicated servers, and female guests will be given long-stemmed red roses for a truly unforgettable dining experience.

Cítricos
DDP: Two credits (T) / Cost: $$$ (TiW)
TYPE: Mediterranean/American; Fine/Signature; Dinner

A word of warning when we talk about Cítricos: since this restaurant prides itself on fresh, seasonally available ingredients, what I'm about to speak of might not be on the menu when you visit. This restaurant takes the buttoned-up class of the Grand Floridian (white linens on the tables) and dresses it down just a smidge with wrought-iron rails (did you know that this is meant to resemble a grape vine?) and mosaic floors. You will have to dress in accordance with the more formal dress code.

You can begin your meal with a cheese course, or start with an appetizer like tuna tartare, chorizo arancini, sweet onion bisque, seasonal flatbread, or pork belly. Entrées include red wine-braised beef short ribs, oak-grilled swordfish, scallop risotto, beef filet, halibut, quinoa and Provençale ratatouille, and chicken Mediterranean. You can enhance any of these meals with pan-seared scallops, mashed potatoes, and crispy brussels sprouts. Disney Check meals are shrimp, grilled chicken breast, beef sirloin steak, and pasta with marinara. Kids can also order mac and cheese, pizza, or a French grilled ham and cheese sandwich. End your meal with refreshing sorbet or gelato, or get the Florida key lime pie or tropical fruit crème brûlée. There are a few specialty cocktails and beers on this menu, but the highlight as far as alcohol goes is the award-winning wine list. The wines are sold by the ounce and use up-to-date technology to preserve the freshness of the pour. Sommeliers are also on hand to make suggestions.

For a truly special experience, sign up to do the Cítricos Chef's Domain, a table for 12 in a private dining area where you can enjoy multiple courses paired with fine wines. Watch your meal being made in the show kitchen, with a dinner that is specifically tailored to your group's palate preferences.

Narcoossee's

DDP: Two credits (T) / Cost: $$-$$$ (TiW)
TYPE: Seafood/American; Fine/Signature; Sunday Brunch and Dinner

Narcoossee's is unlike the other dining options at the Grand Floridian because it isn't housed in the main building. It's out overlooking the water of the Seven Seas Lagoon, making it a sometimes overlooked spot and a bit easier to get a reservation. If you time it right, you'll have a great view of the Electrical Water Pageant and fireworks at the Magic Kingdom, though you must adhere to Disney's formal dress code.

You can begin your meal with Maine lobster bisque, a salad, or try one of the other delicious appetizers like slow-poached and chilled shrimp, calamari, shrimp and grits, shrimp and crab cake, or an artisanal cheese selection served with prosciutto. Main courses include steamed Maine lobster, halibut, salmon, surf and turf, New York strip, wild caught shrimp and campanelle pasta, scallops, filet mignon, and pork tenderloin. Enhance any of these entrées with asparagus, Narcoossee's signature mashed potatoes, brussels sprouts, or béarnaise sauce. The Disney Check meals are grilled chicken breast, veggie burger, oven-roasted wild shrimp, and Mickey pasta with house-made tomato sauce. Other kid's meals include grilled flat iron steak, mac and cheese, burgers, or crispy fried chicken tenders. The desserts are as delectable as the main courses, with options like cheesecake, chocolate torte, Narcoossee's candy bar, mango sorbet, and coconut and chocolate crème brûlée. There are specialty coffee drinks including the Narcoossee's Nutcracker with Kahlúa, Baileys Irish Cream, Frangelico, Skyy Vodka, and whipped cream, or the Nutty Irishman with Baileys Irish Cream and Frangelico topped with whipped cream. You can also order a glass of wine (from their impressive selection!) to complement your steak or seafood dish.

Polynesian Village Resort

'Ohana

DDP: One credit (T) / Cost: $$-$$$ (TiW)
TYPE: Polynesian; Unique/Themed; Breakfast (Character) and Dinner
CHARACTERS (breakfast): Lilo, Stitch, Pluto, Mickey

'Ohana, like Cape May Café and Trattoria Al Forno, only has character dining in the morning for breakfast. You'll meet Lilo, Stitch, Pluto, and Mickey, all decked out in their best luau gear. You might want to plan your Magic Kingdom day around dining at 'Ohana since it's on the monorail loop. Epcot would also be convenient based on the Polynesian's proximity to the Transportation and Ticket Center (which takes you directly to Epcot via monorail). The dining room looks like a Polynesian longhouse with Tiki gods and intricately carved woodwork.

The breakfast menu is simple: eggs, sausage, pineapple-coconut breakfast bread, breakfast potatoes, Mickey waffles, and seasonal fruit served family-style to your table in a skillet.

The characters might leave after breakfast, but the menu selection increases for dinner. You will start with 'Ohana pineapple-coconut bread and a mixed greens salad with a lilikoi dressing. Then for appetizers you'll get a dish of pork dumplings tossed in garlic-ginger sauce (this is the highlight of my meal at 'Ohana) and honey-coriander chicken wings. For entrées, your servers will come around with large skewers of meat: sweet and sour chicken, Szechuan sirloin steak, and spicy grilled peel and eat shrimp. You meal will also have noodles tossed in teriyaki sauce and stir-fried vegetables. End your meal with the famous 'Ohana bread pudding a la mode or, for children, a brownie with marshmallow topping and M&Ms. Since this is all-you-care-to-enjoy, your servers will be circling around your table to see if there's anything else you want. Want more Szechuan sirloin steak and less shrimp? It's no problem, just ask the server.

I've eaten at 'Ohana once for dinner. Maybe my expectations were too high, but I was thoroughly underwhelmed. I found the food and the service to be just okay. If I'm paying nearly $50 for a dinner, I should be blown away by the entrées. My highlight should not be the salad and the pork dumplings.

Disney's Spirit of Aloha Dinner Show

DDP: Two credits (T) / Cost: $$$ (TiW, late show only)
TYPE: Polynesian; Dinner Show; Dinner

The Spirit of Aloha Dinner Show is hidden away in Luau Cove, in the back of the Polynesian on the path to the Grand Floridian. Spirit of Aloha consists of a stage show with family-style dinner service. There are three categories of seats: one (the best, front-row seats) through three (the "cheap" seats with a potentially obstructed view). The show itself consists of island storytelling (with some historical background), hula dancing, and fire-knife dancing. If you've been to a luau in Hawaii or are looking for an authentic luau experience, this is not the same caliber. Let's call this luau-lite. The performances are cancelled if the temperature falls below 50 degrees.

Food-wise, your starters will consist of a tropical mixed greens salad with mango poppy seed dressing, pineapple-coconut bread, and fresh sweet pineapple. Entrées are island barbecue pork ribs, Polynesian rice, and fresh seasonal vegetables. End your dinner with a Kilauea Volcano Delight, a chocolate mousse served with raspberry sauce. Beverages also are all-you-care-to-enjoy: sodas, tea, coffee, milk, lemonade, Bud, Bud Light, Cabernet Sauvignon, and Chardonnay. These are all included with the price of admission.

Wilderness Lodge

Artist Point

DDP: Two credits (T) / Cost: $$$ (TiW)
TYPE: Pacific Northwest/American; Fine/Signature; Dinner

This upscale dining location in Wilderness Lodge serves a hybrid of food from the Pacific Northwest, including Washington, Oregon, and British Columbia. You'll enjoy your meal in an open and airy dining room overlooking the lush foliage of the lodge surrounded by Craftsman-style architecture. Like several of the other signature dining locations on property, your party will have to adhere to the "business casual" dress code while dining at Artist Point.

Start your meal with oysters, tuna tataki, mussels, venison tartare, or build your own charcuterie tray with cheeses and meats. The menu includes butcher cuts with options like a filet, porterhouse, hanger steak, and aged bone-in rib-eye for two. Other entrées are venison, farm egg pappardelle, scallops, salmon, roasted chicken, and wild halibut paella for two. You can enhance any meal with roasted bone marrow, blue cheese, chimichurri, shishito peppers, and horseradish sauce. For the full experience, you can opt to indulge in the Taste of the Pacific five-course meal. It starts with a champagne toast and ends with a dessert. Disney Check entrées are grilled chicken breast and roasted cedar plank salmon. Chicken breast, pasta, and a petit steak are also available on the kid's menu. For dessert, there's warm donuts, almond butter cookies, cobbler, and crème brûlée. There are some regionally appropriate wines, as well as a few themed cocktails like the Lodge Fizz and North Flight Martini.

Disney announced that Artist Point will become a character dining location at the end of 2018. This "Storybook Dining" experience will include visits from Snow White, Grumpy, Dopey, and the Evil Queen. The dinner will be a prix-fixe menu with shared starters.

Whispering Canyon Café

DDP: One credit (T) / Cost: $-$$ (TiW)
TYPE: American; Unique/Themed; Breakfast, Lunch, and Dinner

Whispering Canyon is sandwiched in between Artist Point and Yachtsman Steakhouse in this book. Don't get it confused—Whispering Canyon is not here for fine dining; it's here for unique dining experiences. The café is a rollicking good time with hearty, home-cookin' located in the cavernous lobby of Wilderness Lodge. You might hear it before you see it, because guests are encouraged to have a rootin-tootin' good time. It might be a hobby-horse race, or a race to find a bottle of ketchup, but either way, it's hard to leave without a smile on your face. You won't find Mickey and Minnie here wearing cowboy hats, but you get that same fun experience from your wait staff. This might be a good place to test the waters if you aren't sure your kids are going to be into meeting the costumed characters.

For breakfast, you can get the all-you-care-to-enjoy skillet with scrambled eggs, country potatoes, hickory-smoked bacon, sausage, Mickey waffles, house-made buttermilk-cheddar biscuits, and sausage gravy. You can also order from the menu, with breakfast classics like eggs-any style, banana bread French toast, or a ham and cheddar omelet. Kids can also order the all-you-care-to-enjoy breakfast skillet, steel-cut oatmeal, fruit cup, banana bread French toast, eggs, spinach and tomato omelet (Disney Check), or Mickey waffles. Adults can order mimosas and Bloody Marys with their breakfasts.

There is a lunch version of the all-you-care-to-enjoy skillet, with fresh baked cornbread, slow-smoked pork ribs, barbecued pulled pork, citrus herb chicken, western-style sausage, mashed Yukon potatoes, buttered corn, and cowboy-style baked beans. You'll find other western-inspired menu items here like the chopped bison burger, slow-smoked pulled-pork sandwich, St. Louis-style pork ribs, and skillet-fired quinoa cakes. Add enhancements like baked mac and cheese, turkey-braised greens, and charred ranch broccoli. Disney Check meals are the multigrain grill cheese dipper, grilled chicken breast, and grilled fish of the day. Kids can also order burgers, nuggets, mac and cheese, and their own version of the all-you-care-to-enjoy lunch skillet.

The prices go up a bit for dinner. The all-you-care-to-enjoy skillet for dinner includes family-style mixed greens dressed with apple vinaigrette, fresh-baked cornbread, slow-smoked pork ribs, barbecued pulled pork, citrus herb chicken, oak-smoked beef brisket, western-style sausage, mashed Yukon potatoes, buttered corn, seasonal farm-fresh vegetables, and cowboy-style baked beans. Heartier à la carte items are on the dinner menu like New York strip, braised pork shank, and a full slab of St. Louis-style pork ribs. The kid's meals remain the same at lunch and dinner. You'll find a selection of beer and wine as well as a list of specialty cocktails. Stay in theme with a moonshine margarita, moonshine lemonade, or mountain trail cocktail with moonshine whiskey, Chambord, blackberry brandy, and wildberry topped with lemonade.

Yacht Club Resort

Yachtsman Steakhouse

DDP: Two credits (T) / Cost: $$$ (TiW)
TYPE: Mediterranean/American; Fine/Signature; Dinner

The Yachtsman Steakhouse in located in (no surprises here) the Yacht Club Resort. The spacious dining room is peppered with New England style touches like knotty pine beams and nautical decor. Since this is a fine dining experience, you must adhere to the Disney "business casual" dress code.

Every meal begins with a bread basket. Now, this isn't your ordinary bread basket, because it also comes with butter and a ramekin of roasted garlic. Did I mention there is onion bread, too? Bring mints. The soup and salad menu consists of French Onion soup, lobster bisque, Caesar salad, and the Waldorf wedge salad. Appetizers include shrimp cocktail, artisanal cheeses, crab cake, Moroccan kafta beef blossoms, and a charcuterie board. Be careful not to overeat before your meal, because the entrées are filling and delicious. There are a few seafood options like the Maine lobster, pan-seared sea scallops, or the Yachtsman Seafood Plateau for two complete with broiled Maine lobster, mussels, baked crab cake, snapper ceviche, chilled jumbo shrimp, oysters Rockefeller, and braised sliced octopus. The seafood is great, but the cornerstone of this establishment is the steak. Choose from the Wagyu strip loin, 32-oz porterhouse for two, filet mignon, prime rib, New York strip, or rib-eye. The entrées are not served with any sides, but sides can be ordered family style. Choose from truffle mac and cheese, sautéed mushrooms, beef fat potatoes, roasted asparagus, creamed spinach, braised onions, twice baked potato, glazed carrots, and sweet summer cream corn. Disney Check meals are grilled chicken breast and the baked fish of the day. Kids meals include mac and cheese, orecchiette pasta and meatballs, and oak-grilled steak skewer. For dessert, go light with the sorbet or go all-in with the Admiral's Cake (decadent layered cake of Valrhona chocolate brownie, caramel crunch, dark chocolate ganache, chocolate sponge cake, bananas foster jam, and caramel ganache). Like most other signature restaurants on property, there is an impressive wine list here.

Acknowledgments

Thank you to everyone who offered encouragement and words of kindness during this project. Thanks to Bob McLain for thinking of me. Special thanks to the Gabriels, the Dicksons, the Martyns, the Wozniaks, the LaForgias, the Caseys, Jake, Scott, Amy, Ben, Mindy, Stevie, Breanna, Erin and Joe.

To my parents: you two have given me everything I could have possibly needed to succeed in life, tangible and otherwise. Thank you for everything.

Matt: I truly could not have done this without you. I am sitting here on the day of our anniversary putting the finishing touches on this book. Meanwhile, you've picked up the slack of our life. That's the kind of mensch you are. Consider this book a "Katherine-will-clean-the-house-coupon" of sorts.

About the Author

Katherine Walsh was born and raised in south-central Pennsylvania. She was a Public Relations major at York College of Pennsylvania, where she met her husband, Matt. After they graduated, Katherine got a job with the federal government. Katherine and Matt have two adopted cats, Archie and Matilda.

Katherine's non-travel time is spent doing a variety of extracurriculars. She is an esteemed member of her trivia team. She contributes to the Disney podcast WDW Happy Hour (subscribe today!). She listens to a lot of Weird Al Yankovic, showtunes, and 90s alternative rock. She sings karaoke and plays the ukulele. She drinks wine and acts like a "Real Housewife of York, PA."

Her first book, *Adulting in Disney*, was published by Theme Park Press in 2018.

ABOUT THEME PARK PRESS

Theme Park Press publishes books primarily about the Disney company, its history, culture, films, animation, and theme parks, as well as theme parks in general.

Our authors include noted historians, animators, Imagineers, and experts in the theme park industry.

We also publish many books by first-time authors, with topics ranging from fiction to theme park guides.

And we're always looking for new talent. If you'd like to write for us, or if you're interested in the many other titles in our catalog, please visit:

www.ThemeParkPress.com

• •

Theme Park Press Newsletter

Subscribe to our free email newsletter and enjoy:

- ◆ Free book downloads and giveaways
- ◆ Access to excerpts from our many books
- ◆ Announcements of forthcoming releases
- ◆ Exclusive additional content and chapters
- ◆ And more good stuff available nowhere else

To subscribe, visit www.ThemeParkPress.com, or send email to newsletter@themeparkpress.com.

Read more about these books
and our many other titles at:

www.ThemeParkPress.com

Made in the USA
Columbia, SC
09 May 2019